Sacred ANGER

Sacred ANGER

Uncover the teachings of your most feared emotion

SERYNA MYERS

London

The book information is catalogued as follows;
Author Name(s): Seryna Myers
Title: Sacred Anger: Uncover the teachings of your most feared emotion

1st Edition, 2021

Book Design by Leah Kent
Cover image credit: Jakub Gojda/Shutterstock.com

ISBN (paperback) 978-1-913479-72-5
ISBN (ebook) 978-1-913479-73-2

Published by That Guy's House
www.ThatGuysHouse.com

To R.
Thank you for taking this beautiful, sometimes-uncomfortable journey with me.

It's so much more fun with you by my side.

Thanks for making me feel safe enough to dig into my shadows
and for loving me through the process.

CONTENTS

FOREWORD

I used to think my answer to the question "What animal are you?" was so clever.

A chameleon.

I saw my ability to shift shape for those around me meant I was flexible and easy to get along with, and could fit into any situation. Some of that was true, but I was unaware of the sadness within that declaration.

I wasn't grounded in the truth of who I was. Unapologetically. I didn't even really have a firm grasp of the core of who I was.

I thought I did.

I didn't care where we went to eat. I didn't need to decide for us where we were staying. It didn't matter what movie, what song, what outfit, what time. That's not being wishy washy...that's being flexible. Not controlling. Right?

Oh! You have opinions that are in direct opposition to my core values? No problem. I'm here to respect your opinion.

You are annoyed? I am sorry. So sorry. Seriously. I am really sorry. Can you accept my apology?

What can I change about me, do differently, do for you that will make your life better or more importantly and accurately, like me?

I became a therapist and made a career that allowed me and further trained me in the value and necessity of hiding my thoughts and feelings. I literally perfected the poker face and ability to always see another's perspective.

That isn't to say I didn't have opinions. I wasn't a wallflower.

I had opinions. I was afraid to voice them.

I had feelings. I was reticent to share and create conflict.

I felt pissed off but I was afraid of how I would handle the conflict.

So I bottled it up. It snuck up on me. And my loved ones. And then I blew.

I would say I had a very long fuse hooked up to fireworks. It would go something like: sweet, easy going, sweet then what a fucking mouth and attitude! Does she have an anger issue? Who the hell is that????

Then came the shame. The judgement. Condemnation.

YOU caused this. You are the problem. You have a problem. You need help.

And I did.

Telling me I had an issue with anger didn't land. It didn't speak to my truth. It didn't inform me in a way that inspired me to face myself. To take a good hard look at why I behaved the way I did.

I didn't have an anger issue.

I had an issue with anger.

I had two seminal moments that changed my perspective with anger.

I had a treasured mentor, June, who was my confidant and life Sherpa for a period of my life. I spoke with her about the relationships in my life that vexed me. A controlling family member. An addicted relationship partner. A dominating friend. I painted myself as the victim. I was certain I was a victim. She heard me out.

And then loving kicked my ass.

She told me what they did was awful. Horrible. It made sense for me to be devastated. To be angry. To feel rage.

She told me that she would feel the same way but she would never act like I did.

Dagger.

I felt judged. Shut down and misunderstood, and like I had very much picked the wrong mentor.

She continued.

She told me to see the value in my feelings towards the people who made me angry and their behavior, but I didn't have a right to scorch the village with my anger.

I didn't see another way.

It felt justified. It felt like the ONLY reaction. "I can't see how anyone would react any differently!" I declared with a righteous tone and through burning tears.

She said...."Choose to react to your feelings differently. See your feelings as warning signals, not a means to finally release the perspectives you hold in." She warned me that raging in response to unjust behavior wounded my soul much more than it would teach the other person to treat me differently, or change the situation to be what I want.

And she was right.

The way I dealt with my anger rarely resulted in what I wanted. I may have rattled off some long held 'truths' to someone and released my stress but mainly I just fed righteousness that was off-putting and made it easy to dismiss my points and personhood.

This began an important shift with anger. I realized I needed to nurture and grow a relationship with all my feelings, but especially anger.

The second moment was during the very contentious dissolution of my marriage. After years of betrayal and abuse, I filed for divorce. During the grueling process, I discovered that my ex had been recording conversations between us.

My lawyer called me and said, "I have to warn you. He's made many recordings of you two. You aren't going to like hearing them but you need to sit with all 7 hours of them.

Recordings? What?

I tried to search through my memory of what he could possibly have recorded. I couldn't remember anything that would make me look bad, or that I'd be afraid to have out in the world. I hadn't done anything wrong in our marriage so what could he possibly have recorded... Let alone 7 hours of it?

So I sat down one day and listened.

To all 7 hours of him turning on the recording after baiting me on a topic of conflict. I don't know if you've ever heard yourself pissed off, righteous or letting someone who has wronged you have it, but I can say I have now.

And it wasn't fun.

I heard my hurt and devastation. I heard indignation.

It wasn't all yelling but sometimes it was. I cussed a lot. I said some searing truths.

I had bold silences.

I heard 7 whole hours of me being really angry.

It wasn't a fair reflection of our relationship. He knew he was recording so he behaved and performed for it. I felt safe enough to let it go because he was finally 'hearing me out' and 'letting me unload it all onto him'.

I processed it from a legal perspective as my lawyer instructed, and there was nothing of note within any of it. In the end, not a minute of it was used in court.

But after listening to it all... I had a sick feeling in my soul.

It was ugly.

All that pain and anger and loss and madness. I didn't know where to begin and how to process it.

I remember one of my lawyers talking to me about the things my ex had done during our marriage. She said "I can't believe you handled it as well as you did. Most women would have lost their shit a lot more."

But now here it was: my anger. On display. A legal strategy. Positioned as out of control and controlling.

I was angry that I'd been set up. Betrayed.

I was angry the justice system allowed it, and that a lawyer like my ex's existed.

I was angry I had married him. I was angry I had stayed with him.

I was angry about 100 things and I had no idea what to do with it because anger was dangerous. It was unpredictable. It had consequences, and now my anger was being used as a weapon against me. By two white men - and that made me angry too.

As a therapist and counselor, it can be difficult to find someone who you can put aside your expert status to, and receive wisdom and insight. I'm fortunate because I found this person as a friend and colleague. Seryna Myers.

I went to Seryna after this and she gave me a beautiful talking to. About anger. She said something that set me on a path of healing and understanding.

She told me that my anger was sacred. It stopped me in my tracks.
Intrigued... Tell me more.

My takeaway was this:

- I was afraid of anger in others. (I had experienced brutal domestic violence and emotional manipulation.)

- I was afraid of anger in myself. (I was aware of what I sounded like when I finally hit my breaking point.)

- I didn't know how to 'anger'. I didn't know

or understand the concept of the VERB anger. (I recognized it took me a long time to GET angry and thought the fact that I wasn't a quick trigger meant I 'knew how to anger'.)

- I didn't know the sacred place anger had in my healing, insight and self-development. (Well, this was just a game changing concept.)

Seryna walked me through the origin, purpose and importance of my anger. She shared stories of her own. She normalized it. She helped put words to the way society described anger - especially in women.

She walked me through a purposeful journey that helped me see anger as a helpful tool in my life. To make peace with it, and to process its presence as something that was a gift and not a weapon.

My shame dissipated.

My reactiveness lessened.

I faced my anger. I thanked it and I made it one of the most sacred parts of me.

She's gifted like that, Seryna is. She has this beautiful mixture of bad ass Oh No She Didn't, Let Me Tell You Truths with this gorgeous soft, compassionate container of support. She is special. She is the kind of friend you hope for, and the sort of colleague you long for. Seryna has walked the walk and knows how to shoot it straight. You believe her because she's been there. She's earned my respect tenfold as I've observed her for years being a person of integrity that is real and full of insight.

Seryna saw the crying collective wound we have right now, caused by our inexperience with constructive and sacred anger. Seryna found the perspective and prescription to a society that is desperate to understand what to do with our anger, how to handle others' anger and why sacred anger is the game changer threaded throughout all of it.

Dr. Juliana Hauser
(S)expert, Therapist, Speaker, Author

PROLOGUE

"YOU'RE writing a book about anger?"

My shadow self is a bit of a dick. She has this voice that drips of sneers and jeers, and she has this perfect ability to push on the most sensitive of my buttons.

And in a sense... she was right.

I'm not a therapist, I'm not a neurologist, and I'm not a researcher, so who am I to write this book, right?

But here's how she's wrong...

As a sacred soul mentor and lightworker, I'm committed to creating safe spaces for inner work and supporting people as they shine the light into their own shadows. But beyond my work, this is something I do each and every day for myself. I've transformed my early life filled with chaos, uncertainty, and instability into a livelihood of trust, confidence and hope. I'm committed to this work, and to learning from this sacred teacher.

Yup, I said sacred.

When we approach anything with love, curiosity, and a willingness to challenge our own beliefs about it, we allow the divine to work through it. This could be anything as simple as washing the dishes, to the bigger exploration of an emotion like anger (or joy, or bliss – but those are conversations for other books). When divine light is shining into anything, we develop a relationship with it, it shows us new facets of ourselves, we bring presence and mindfulness into that moment, and THAT my friend is when the magic happens.

Suddenly anger is no longer a temper tantrum, or an outburst. It becomes the way that we're moving energy, we're releasing something deep and aching within us that needed to be expressed. Then in the aftermath, we can be with that energy and reflect on what had us so triggered, what was going on beneath the surface, why it mattered so much... and then we grow from it.

While it would be great to tell you that the end

goal is to become the master of your anger so that you never experience it, I'd like to set some realistic goals for you. What you'll find as you work with anger is not that you don't get angry, but that you get a better grasp on how you react to it. And that comes with a lot of time, inner work, and self mastery. For most of us, the feelings themselves don't go away, but how you handle them, and how quickly you recover from them, will change.

So while it may seem cheeky to ask, since we've only just met, can we make a commitment to each other?

We're right at the beginning of a really exciting journey together, and I want to make sure we step out on a solid foundation.

Let's have some real, honest conversations. With each other. With ourselves.

Because you'll notice that I said we're at the beginning of a really exciting journey, but I made zero promise that it would be an easy one. Sometimes it will be easy. Sometimes, while reading this book, you're going to have the big epiphanies and heart opening realizations or rememberings that will make you delighted to read this book.

But sometimes, the realness will also be a bit tough.

We're going to be exploring the many facets of anger, and it's going to make you realize some uncomfortable things. You're going to look at some stuff you've been actively avoiding and you may find yourself needing to make some changes you've known were coming but that you didn't feel ready for.

There will be times when I'm going to make you mad, and it will be super easy for you to project everything you're feeling onto me. And while the very human part of me wants you to like me, I know that pushing you is essential for your growth. Please know too that all the feelings this book may bring up for you are completely valid, totally normal, and a natural part of the process. The important thing is that you just. Keep. Going.

Breathe.

Back when I was 27, I started a year of self-reflection where I started to become really aware of how negative, critical, and judgmental the little voice in my head was. I was presented with a really unique opportunity to work with a shaman to work through all of the contributing factors that lead to my inner voice being such a bitch, and it took me a year and a half to find the courage to take the first step to working through my stuff. So trust me when I say I know how easy it is to avoid dealing. But please also know how great it can be on the other side, once you start doing the work. My journey began before modern technology made distraction available on every smartphone. Social media, Netflix, games, and the rapidly changing news cycle are all available in your pocket, making it easy to tune in so you can tune out. I'm going to encourage you to try something else.

Because here's the thing about inner work: once you know, you can't un-know. Opening this book means you've started the journey. That your heart said yes. And maybe how fast you walk will vary depending on what parts you're sifting through, and what it's bringing up for you, but you're still moving forward and that's what counts.

So coming back to commitment...

I'm asking for you to see this through. Read all the way to the end. If it becomes too much and you need to put it down, that's totally okay. It's important for you to honour your process, and to give yourself the space to work through whatever comes up. The commitment I'm asking from you is that you see things through to the end. And to be honest, I really hope this book isn't your last stop on the self-reflection train. I want this to inspire you to dig deeper, to want more, and to give yourself permission to create an abundant life you love.

My commitment to you in this book is to keep asking the questions.

My superpower is in holding sacred space where people can have honest conversations with themselves. This book is full of intuitively guided questions to help you tap into the parts of yourself that have previously gone unexplored, so please trust that you're holding this book in your hands now because you're ready to ask them.

And while I know that reading a book isn't the same as working with me one on one you are always welcome to join my online community, The Lightwalker's Path where you'll find people on a similar journey as you. We're better together, and your journey is worthy of a bit of extra love and support.

With love and magic,

PS: I wanted to expand the teachings within this book from the theoretical to the experiential, so here's how you can get the most out of this book:

1) Each chapter ends with a few questions to bring into your reflection process. Grab your favourite journal (or the Sacred Anger companion journal) so you have somewhere to dig into these questions.

2) Head over to sacredangerbook.com and sign up for additional downloadable resources to support your journey.

3) Share your biggest takeaways on social media and tag me @serynamyers in your posts so I can celebrate your wins.

Part 1
Accepting Anger

CHAPTER 1
So, you're angry...

Throughout this book we're going to explore the many faces of anger - because sometimes it's a convenient mask for something bigger and, if you can believe it, more uncomfortable. But that's only some of the time.

There are some legitimate things to be pissed off about in this world too.

At the time I'm writing this book, I've witnessed some massive steps backwards in human rights, racial and gender equality, and the battle to protect the environment. People are in positions of power who are corrupt, and who carry unchecked biases. People who regard countries and policies as business decisions that put profit before people. We've lost sight of the things that really matter. The little guy feels invisible, voiceless. The ones who try to use their voices are silently screaming because they've become so hoarse from shouting for and demanding change from every rooftop and soap box.

There's some epic shifts and scientific and technological advancements happening, but it's also a really challenging time right now. So let's explore that.

You're not happy and you feel powerless to change it.

At home, you find yourself in the endless cycle of dishes piling up, picking up people's socks, and trying to keep everyone in your family looking at least semi-presentable. And God-only-knows what the neighbours are saying about your lawn. It's an endless cycle of trying to keep up, trying to have enough energy for it all, and feeling pretty unappreciated through the entire process. There's increased insomnia, increased mental health struggles, increased household debt. But this is happiness, right? This is success?

At work, there are deadlines looming, unreasonable bosses, windowless cubicles, and long, thankless hours with a boring commute. (You try to use the time for self improvement, listening to inspirational stories on Audible and podcasts, but even those a-ha moments aren't enough to make it all feel worthwhile.) There's work that needs to be done but isn't especially fulfilling. There's complaints, there's a pressure to do more with less, and budget cuts that make most of it pretty untenable. And while it would be nice to say "forget this!" and chuck your papers in the air in your dramatic exit, there's also the reality of paying bills, feeding your family, and trying to sustain some sort of life in modern society that makes that unlikely. So the pressure builds, the frustration builds, the resentment builds, and you start finding yourself working for the weekend. (If you've ever uttered the phrase "fri-yay", I see you and I forgive you.)

Social movements protesting police violence, lack of gun control, and white supremacism are being ignored. Marriage equality and women's reproductive rights have taken a decades-long step back in some parts of the first world. There is still descrimination about who you love or how you identify - despite it being no one's business but your own. There's climate change, the dying of once thriving species, increased pollution, and way too much plastic.

It can be a scary time to be alive. You have every right to be pissed off.

Whether you're experiencing these frustrations, biases, stigmas and so on, or you're just living in an era where this tension is brewing, there's a thickness and a pressure in the air that wasn't there before, or certainly wasn't as prevalent, and it's not a lot of fun to navigate.

It's big stuff.
It's hard stuff.
It doesn't seem to be changing any time soon. (In fact, I believe it's going to get worse before it can get better.)
It doesn't seem like any one person can do anything to make it matter.

And that's ANGERING.

Because when things are hard, we don't want to drown in them, we want to learn to swim. If dog paddling doesn't work, we want to try the breast stroke. We need to feel like agents of change in our lives, like change is even possible so that we can ride out the hard times. "This too shall pass" isn't enough to weather the storm. We need to know that, worst case scenario, we can find an umbrella.

You've been denying how you feel.

The old pattern is to tune out and numb out. It

can be Netflix, food, sex, alcohol and drugs, work, or compulsively cleaning the house. Anything to give the appearance (to ourselves as much as anyone else) that everything is fine, it's under control, and in fact, we're thriving.

But when we tune out and numb out, we're anything but fine. We're avoiding our shit, and it's not like it just passes without us - it's waiting for us as soon as we stop. And... we have to stop eventually.

So when you've reached the last ever episode of Stranger Things, and your problems are hanging out waiting for your attention (and have worsened because they weren't dealt with when they initially came up), what are you going to do?

Anxiety and overwhelm are certainly an option. But we can strive for better than that, can't we?

You never learned how to deal with your emotions.

Young boys all over have been told that emotions like sadness, vulnerability, and fear are weak, are feminine, and that they have to man up in order to deal. Anger is acceptably masculine, so long as it is controlled, and not used to scare or intimidate.

Young girls all over have been told that emotions like sadness, vulnerability, and fear are too much, and over dramatic, and that they need to tone it down or they'd never find a husband. (Leaving out their value being tied up with finding a spouse, but that's a whole other conversation.) Anger is decidedly "not nice" and should be avoided at all times, lest they're found to be considered too butch, or too bitchy, and therefore undesirable.

Let's call bullshit on all of that.

There's a cool thing that's happening right now. Conscious living, including emotional awareness, has been going mainstream. There are more books being written, more blogs and podcasts (including mine) dedicated to what it means to live an intuitive or spiritual life, and websites like Goop.com (and their Netflix special) have brought these concepts into the homes of women who may not have come across it before.

Some people who've been on the conscious living train for awhile really turn up their noses at it becoming a bandwagon to jump on and have mastered the art of a sarcastic eye roll when someone newer to the path talks about how they are living more mindfully.

I think it's great.

Because we all start somewhere. But also with woo-ful living becoming more mainstream, more conversations are happening. We are not just raising consciousness, we are becoming more conscious, more mindful of the impact of our words, of how we need to challenge the status quo, or how we can rewrite the programming we've been given. This current generation are the parents of tomorrow, which means we're raising kids to live more consciously. We're leading by example, finding new ways to express our emotions in healthy and constructive ways, and doing away with labelling them by any sort of gender. We find supportive, sacred, and productive ways to navigate what we feel, and we're teaching them to do the same.

We often think of our inner work as being a benefit for ourselves and, yeah, we are the ones reaping the immediate benefits. We're finding ways to lift the emotional burden of our childhood programming. We're shedding the layers of inherited shame, stigma, limiting beliefs, feeling more freedom than was ever possible for our predecessors. We are our ancestors' wildest dreams rendered corporeal. When we let things go, in every sense, the releases we do don't just benefit us, even though that's the most obvious expression of it. It frees those who came before, it clears our lineage so the inherited patterns stop repeating themselves, which not only frees our children and future grandchildren on an energetic level, they're watching us living, honouring, expressing our heart's truth - the good, the bad, the ugly - in healthy, helpful and restorative ways, so they can do the same. We are living examples of what is possible, and that we can disrupt the status quo.

This, I believe, is what will save our future.

We've put ourselves and the fate of the human race and the planet in the hands of a new generation of children who embody consciousness on a cellular and physical level. In just one generation, enough will shift that we will know what to do with ourselves. We will connect to ourselves, our faith, and each other with new depth, new honesty. It will be safe to be vulnerable, to be hopeful. Anger will be seen as a teacher, as something that is experienced, not as an identity, not as something to fear. It's raw, unbridled truth that will be channeled for good.

We're heading in the right direction.

You never learned to make change.

Changemaking is a brave and sometimes lonely task. It requires a willingness to risk, to get things wrong. It means disrupting the status quo which rocks the boat and sometimes makes people uncomfortable - yourself included. It means putting up your money, your time, your energy, your hope with no guaranteed payoff. It sometimes means going it alone, which leaves you feeling rejected, abandoned, lonely.

So why on earth would anyone bother?

Not changing means stagnation. It means surrendering the keys to the car that you navigate life from, and permanently choosing to ride in the backseat, watching life pass you by. It means no matter how powerless you feel, or how angry, or how hungry for more (or different) you may become, that you must sit back and coast, letting those around you dictate what your life will look like.

Changemakers are shit disturbers.

It's a lot easier to control people who aren't willing to risk it all, which maintains the current power dynamic. We see this on bigger scales like our governments, but it also happens in the microsystems of our families and communities.

How often do you see people wanting to make big changes dismissed? In our social circles, visionary isn't a word you'll see thrown around often (even when it's merited), but Arrogant is. It's a lot easier to dismiss someone as being delusional, power-hungry, or out of touch with reality when their desire for change challenges our comfort with staying the same. But it doesn't make their desire for better invalid.

When was the last time you examined the things that make you angry? I'd be willing to bet that at the root of them there's a desire for things to be different, and perhaps even an underlying belief that they never will be. You can use these questions to help you dig into your current levels of discomfort to make change something that's possible, even on a small (but buildable) scale.

What's making me angry?
What needs to change (within me, or externally)
for me to feel differently?
Do I believe this is possible? Why/why not?
What supports do I need to make this change?
(If I don't know, who can I ask or
what research can I do to find out?)
What kind of timeline does this need?
What next steps am I willing to commit to today?

When we start to get honest with what's underneath what we're feeling, we're empowered to back it with a plan. Then whatever anger is left becomes fuel to move things forward rather than the very emotion that holds you back and keeps you stuck.

You never learned to accept consequences without shame.

I come from a family of blamers. We were raised to not apologize, to not take the blame, and to dodge consequences at any cost. When our actions caused consequences, it was always someone else's fault. I'll give you an example.

In the summer of 1998, there was an attempted drug raid on our family home. I'd moved away two weeks before, and my family had been camping at the time, so nothing was found, and no arrests were made. My family immediately began suspecting friends and neighbours as "rats", rather than looking at the possible contributions that would've led to a raid in the first place. I'll be honest: everything wasn't entirely on the up and up, and the police's warrant was likely valid. It was easier to name and blame than it was to admit that we should have been doing things differently.

It wasn't until a few years later when I worked for a manager who valued the ability to accept personal responsibility above all else that I even realized I did this. I started looking back at every relationship I had, every work conflict, every teacher I'd been mad at. I'd blamed them for a bad grade because it was hard to admit I'd slacked and half-assed an assignment.

And that's with only the socio-economic cards being stacked against me. As an able-bodied, educated white woman, I still carried a lot of privilege that is denied to so many. The responsibility I've been asked to take in my lifetime has largely been mine to take anyways.

Other people have been burdened with presumption and prejudice that we're not even starting from the same place.

Taking personal responsibility, and the consequences that come with it means having honest conversations with ourselves, and we're not given the tools to do that. Without the tools, one of two things happens:

We just can't see our fuck ups.

No matter which way we look at it, it's someone else's fault. If we're able to see the role we played in it, we find loopholes like a bad night's sleep, childhood trauma, a stressful day, a headache. Sure, those are valid things that will impact how we conduct ourselves in the world, but at the end of the day, regardless of what's happened or happening, we are the only ones responsible for our actions. And that my friend, is an inconvenient truth.

We see our fuck ups, and immediately slide down the shame spiral.

The flipside is when we're reading the books or attending the seminars and we have these lightbulb moments where we can see we're responsible, but we're not working with a trained professional like a licensed therapist, we can immediately jump on the shame train. When this happens we often take on not only our own responsibility, but that of everyone else. We become martyrs, burning ourselves at the stake. The behaviour not only makes us feel shittier, it also makes it harder to move ourselves forward because we don't respond well to things that feel bad.

It's important to be honest about the roles we play in our lives, in the good stuff and the bad stuff, but instead of beating ourselves up for it, we have deep self-compassion. Instead of self-flagellation, we can ask questions like:

- Now that I know better, how can I do better next time?
- Who did I hurt? How can I make it up to them?
- How can I show myself more compassion for my humanness?

Brené Brown says that each of us is doing our best at any given time. So it's time to cut ourselves some slack. Even if today's best isn't as good as yesterday's best. We're all just finding our way.

You haven't defined happiness for yourself.

One of the biggest lies we've been told is that there's a one-size-fits-all approach to happiness and success. We go to school, we get married, we start a career, we have kids, buy a house with white picket fence and a dog... and then we wait for retirement.

I can't tell you the number of people I know who only truly start living when they're retired. And what happens to all the ones who retire but don't have the financial means to build the life of their dreams? Or the ones who pass before their time, and never get to truly live?

Building a life on someone else's terms is a recipe for a boatload of resentment.

No one can tell you what you need to be happy. Not your parents, your church, or society.
Not the magazines, Hollywood or the ads you read.
Not the blogs you read, Instagram feeds you follow, or the emails you subscribe to.

You, and only YOU can decide. And once you realize that, a lot will shift. You stop resenting the time you've lost, and the people who influenced you to do things differently. You stop trying to fix everything with another workshop or online course, and start turning inward to find the answers you seek. You stop looking at all the things that you think are robbing you of your joy and start finding the things that bring joy instead.

Stop focusing on everything that makes you mad. Start figuring out what you need to live a vibrant and happy life and then go get it, beauty.

Permission to be pissed off

No matter what you've been told by your parents, your ex-lovers, or your former friends, let me make something clear…

You are entitled to want what you want, need what you need, and feel what you feel.

Go back and read that as many times as necessary for it to sink in. If you're a recovering people pleaser like I am, once just won't be enough.

Your needs, wants, and feelings may not be convenient, accepted, or provided by others, and this will make them a bit uncomfortable, but that doesn't make their existence any less valid.

Here's the thing, lovely: your feelings, no matter how they make people feel, are valid. No one has the right to diminish how you feel, what you've experienced, or the impact events in your life have had on you. Even if it's just in the privacy of your own heart, please know that to be true.

That being said, the needs, wants, and feelings of the people around you are equally valid, and may sometimes clash with your own, so sometimes there needs to be some compromise. What you choose to do with those feelings will have an impact on those around you, and you need to be prepared for what that looks like. This isn't said as some sort of way to silence you, or make you fear speaking up, or taking action, it's just the reality of things. So often books will tell you to follow your heart, and take leaps of faith, but they neglect to tap into the realities of living in this world. Actions have reactions – and it's totally okay, you just need a plan for them.

Anger is one of those emotions that makes

people so uncomfortable, and they'll do almost anything to avoid having to deal with your expression of it. They'll use shame to get you to pipe down (oftentimes because whatever they've done to awaken the anger is likely making them feel shamed too, but they probably don't know that). They'll avoid you until they think you've calmed down. Sometimes this is done with a genuine desire to give you space and privacy to process, but it's usually rooted in their own inability to withstand the discomfort of someone else's anger. Don't take it personally – you'll see this a lot in people who are also really uncomfortable with their own as well. They'll respond in anger (remember, their feelings are valid too), sometimes as an attempt to be the bigger, louder, scarier voice in the room so they don't have to feel silenced, beat down, or victimized, but often because they have their own perspective of things and haven't found a healthy way to channel it yet. That being said, your safety is always at the forefront, so don't let the validity of someone else's feelings put you in danger.

Needless to say, your approach matters. What you choose to do with your anger can really rewrite your experience with it. My father is an

alcoholic, so he can tend to be a bit unpredictable. One minute you're having a seemingly interesting conversation and debate, and then suddenly, it's impossible to agree to disagree, and you're in an argument. His father was the same way, only more so. Growing up with this history of unconstructive, explosive, and unpredictable anger made me fear it, big time. I worried relationships would end if I expressed un
 with something. (And sometimes they did.) I worried it wasn't safe to be around anger (both of my brothers were wall punchers, and holes around the house were commonplace for us).

Mostly though, I feared my own anger. I used to have nightmares about uncontrollable rage, so vivid that I'd wake up in a sweat with a racing heart, and it took a while to realize that something violent hadn't just happened. I feared the damage I could do with my words because as an intuitive, I had a knack for knowing what someone's weak spot was and I didn't trust my anger not to use it.

Here's the good thing though... with time, a lot of inner work, some therapy, and a lot of energetic support, I started to get comfortable with my anger. It became my teacher, and my emotional barometer. Anger would show up as a sign that I hadn't been upholding my boundaries or valuing myself, and it was time to make some shifts to recalibrate. I learned how to express my anger (and other feelings) healthily so that I could honour my needs, wants, and feelings, without harbouring resentment, or feeling physically sick from stuffing them down. And I married a man who not only honours my feelings too, but makes me feel safe to express them, something I'd never had in a partnership before.

When I needed it, anger became my fuel. Rather than slipping into despair when things felt too big, or impossible, anger, and if I'm honest, stubbornness would help me dig in and strategize. The expression is "Where there's a will, there's a way" but my lived experience was "When there's anger, I'll find a way". Anger is what had me write letters to politicians and customer service departments. It's what pushed me to defend myself in court when every part of me wanted to bury my head in the sand and avoid. It's what helped me move out, at the age of 17, with very little support and resources, because my life literally depended on it. And I'm far from the only one. So many activists, politicians, non profit workers are fueled by the things that make their blood boil, and they use that to make some changes in whatever way is possible for them, rather than just posting angrily on Facebook about it.

This intimate relationship with anger allowed me to understand it in newer, deeper ways. It's why I'm able to write this book. When we can step back and look at anger as something to learn from and embrace, rather than something to avoid or suppress, we find out just how much it's capable of. We became partners, anger and I. And we're doing a lot of good in the world, together.

SACRED SOUL SEARCHING

Here are the reflection questions to take
to your journal:

*What is it about my own anger that makes
me so uncomfortable, and where else has
this shown up in my life?*

*What can I learn from the discomfort
that anger (my own, or other people's)
makes me feel?*

CHAPTER 2
Why you're not talking about it

They say holding onto anger is like drinking poison and waiting for the other person to die. If holding our anger in is literally poisoning us, why on Earth aren't we talking about it? Why could it possibly be worth holding it in? Let's press pause on the shame game for a second and explore the many reasons for holding in your anger.

You don't know how to express it constructively.

Anger is an emotion that makes people uncomfortable, and they start to train us out of it when we're pretty young. Women are told that it's not nice, and our niceness is so entwined with being accepted, desired, and "marriage material" that we don't want to jeopardize our place in the community. On the flip side, anger isn't discouraged in men, but they're not taught healthy ways to express their emotions - anger included. I grew up in a pretty angry home, with my brothers punching holes in the walls and lashing out at everyone around them. Let's be honest: just because we're pushing our anger down, doesn't mean it doesn't come out... it means it comes out without our control or say so.

So what does a healthy expression of anger look like? I believe it's expressing things when they're small, before they get a chance to compound (causing death by a thousand cuts). This helps us not build up resentment, and really deals with the root cause of the anger. Have you ever tried to drink a cup of tea that's been oversteeped? Bitter af. That's what happens when you let the little things marinate and fester.

It's also having an outlet. Sometimes that's talk therapy, or a good friend to confide in, but oftentimes the outlet should be physical. Anger is the kind of emotion that needs to move, it needs to be expressed, and physical activity is a great way to help it move through you, instead of consuming you from the inside out. I know a lot of people think the only way to express anger physically is to hit a punching bag - and if that works for you, awesome. But it can also be a really primal dance where you're so in your body and allowing every emotion to run through you. It can be screaming into a pillow and allowing yourself to release with every cell of your being. It can be running, or lifting, or cycling... it doesn't need to be aggressive, it just needs to get the blood flowing and feel good to you. What you do isn't as important as doing something, and being intentional about why you're doing it.

You don't feel safe to express it.

This reason has a couple of pieces. There is a feeling of being unsafe which is rooted in the acceptance piece from before, of being cast out because expressing anger is "not nice". If that's the case, you'll first want to connect with your heart and do some soul searching around why you believe this to be true. This isn't to say that it isn't, when we have these beliefs we often have anecdotal evidence to back them up, but we need to understand where our stories come from. I will say this though, my sweet: your happiness is infinitely more important than someone else's comfort. So if holding in anger is keeping you from being happy, it's time to rock some boats.

Another facet of this fear is when you don't trust yourself to express it safely. This can be because you never learned how to healthily express your feelings, maybe you grew up around a lot of hostility and you've never witnessed a productive way of dealing with anger. Maybe you're working through your own anger and impulsivity and you're afraid of what you're capable of. There are tools that you can learn with the help of trained professionals that will not just help you manage and express the anger itself, but to cultivate the trust within yourself that you'll know what to do when the feelings rise up.

I have a little story for you. When I was 10 years old, my step dad Rick wanted nothing but to be the best dad he could for me. I loved him, but it created a lot of confusion in my heart because my dad was still around, and I felt like loving Rick was betraying my dad. I remember going on a walk with Rick, and telling him that I didn't need him to be my dad, I just wanted to be his friend. None of it was said with malice, my 10 year old self was just trying to make sense of a complicated, far-too-grown-up situation, and she did the best she could to honour her feelings. Rick was hurt though, and he shut down. In the years that followed our relationship wasn't just disconnected, it was cold, sometimes critical. He didn't have the tools to deal with those feelings and he spent years acting out these feelings of hurt and rejection. What I learned from that was that my words were powerful, and I was capable of immense harm, even without trying. It's taken my entire adult life to learn to express certain feelings, even with my own child. My coping strategy was to be cold and cut off until I calmed down because I didn't trust myself to not get it wrong, and I didn't want to say something that would do irreparable damage. I've had to work on this though, because as we got to the more strained parts of my son's teenage years, I realized that I was acting out that same distance I experienced with Rick, and the last thing I wanted my son to feel was that I wasn't a safe space. It's been a constant process of unlearning, and re-learning for me.

Lastly, there are some cases where it is physically not safe for you to express your anger, even in the healthiest, most constructive ways. I'm not a therapist, so this next piece is said with love and compassion but without professional authority... If you are in a space, a relationship, a home where it is not safe for you to express your anger because harm will come your way, it's time to start planning your next steps.

Anger is a normal, natural emotion, and one that will come up from time to time, often rightfully so. You are worthy of feeling safe and secure, no matter what emotion arises. And you are entitled to feel whatever is coming up for you as a result. If the space you're in can't support that, it's time to find one that can. Whether it's help from a friend, a counsellor, a crisis line, a shelter, there is someone locally who can help you. You don't have to do this alone.

You're afraid of being a "too" girl

Hi, I'm Seryna, and I'm a recovering "too" girl. I grew up hearing that I talk too much, I'm too bossy, I'm too emotional, and I'm too sensitive. It wasn't until my 30s that I even realized those things were my super powers.

I talk a lot – but my storytelling is funny and relatable and helps people realize they're not alone in this world because they've felt or experienced the same things. I can't tell you how important it is to me to share my stories so that others don't feel like they're alone. In the darkest nights of my soul I really felt abandoned, and I felt that whatever I was feeling (depression, anxiety, frustration, loss of hope) was a unique experience that no one else could relate to. The more I started to share my journey, the more I found out just how common these things were. As I spoke about it, others came forward and said "I thought I was the only one." Our pain may not define us, but it does sometimes unite us - and if no one talks about it, how can we find each other?

I am literally bossy - I am my own boss, I run my own business as a one-woman-show, and without me, nothing would move forward. I bring vision and inspiration to the table, and then I find ways to make it happen. We need people like that in the world, the ones who take action and who rally others to do the same. Otherwise we'd be living in a sea of grey, without much excitement or innovation ever.

And yeah, I feel things deeply. I've been diagnosed with depression, and prescribed medication to help me manage my mood - and sometimes that includes anger. But can we be real for a second here? It's not like there's some unit of measure where we can define something as the "right amount" of emotions. This isn't a cake we're baking ("I need 2 cups of joy, and a ¼ cup of anger") this is real life. I'd take my ability to feel in excess over being numbed out (by conditioning or as a coping technique) any day. It's all I know. But if I'm entirely honest, this one one of the areas I've had to do a lot of work. And it's ongoing. In my corporate days, the owner of the company nicknamed me "little ball of rage" because I hadn't learned to cope with stressful environments and unreasonable deadlines and expectations. I hadn't learned how to ask for help either. Time, maturity, communication and healthy boundaries helped me develop this area a bit more, and now I have some coping techniques that help me dissipate my anger when it comes up. But let me be clear: that doesn't mean I don't get angry.

I identify as an Empath and, to be honest, I think all children are born empathic and life will dictate how in tune with this gift they remain. In my case, a challenging childhood asked me to stay highly tuned to the emotions and energies around me, purely for my safety. People who've had quite spiritual upbringings would've had these gifts encouraged in different (and more supportive) ways, but the end result is the same: a heightened awareness of the energies and emotions of others. The trick is being able to discern what is yours, and what belongs to someone else so you can behave accordingly.

I've put my sensitivity to work – it's directly connected to my intuitive gifts. My ability to be open, to feel deeply, and to sense how others are feeling is what allows me to tap in and bring the wisdom forward that's in support of someone's highest good and truth. When I didn't know how to cope with this, I experienced burnout, and energetic co-dependence that drained me. But like with everything else, with a bit of support and some coping strategies, I got to leverage the best of my sensitivity and manage the rest.

All of this to say: there is nothing wrong with being too-anything. Too picky, too strict, too focused, too loud... the right people will see how these things are gifts. Feel, be, and embrace all that you are, and surround yourself with those who love you for it (notice I didn't say "in spite of it"). Don't let the fear of being too much keep your voice silent in the world, when it's so badly needed, especially now. Your anger can be fuel – look at the social justice activists who are fighting for equality (for women, for people of colour, for the LGBTQ+ community, and so on). Look at the teachers who strike for better working conditions so they can best serve our children. Look at the scientists and doctors who are driven to find ways to heal because they lost someone close to them and are angry about it, and want to spare anyone from feeling that ever again. If these people didn't use their rage for good, where would we be?

You're afraid you'll go "dark side".

We all have concern about what would happen if we really let it all out... who would get hurt? Who would we become? Can you ever go back? Everything we see in the movies tells us that once we cross that line we can never go back, and while that may be true of some lines, with some humility, sincerity, and genuine apologies, many times reparations can still be made.

Every new day is an opportunity to try things differently. So if you didn't manage your anger, lashed out at the people around you and acted like an asshole today – what are you going to do about it tomorrow? Burying your feelings doesn't change the fact that you're feeling them, and you can only deny things for so long. Typically, the burying is more likely to cause the explosions, than just dealing with things as they are, when they come up, in the first place. Not getting it right every single time, doesn't mean you're not a good person… it means you've got to wake up and try to do better next time. And this may mean getting some help or learning some new skills to get you there.

None of this would even be an issue if we were taught how to express our less-than-sparkly feelings in healthy and constructive ways in the first place. Or if we started dealing with them when they were mild annoyances, instead of marinating in low grade rage until we burst. As adults, we need to take responsibility for ourselves, and our feelings, which doesn't mean shoving them down, but finding a healthy outlet for them, and coping strategies to manage things within ourselves. Would it be nice if our parents, our cultures, the media and society did a better job to condition us to know what to do? Absolutely. But if that's not the case (and let's be honest, it's not the case), then it's up to us to say, "Okay, cool, now what do I do?" instead of just blowing up and blaming it on not having learned how to manage things better.

Only villains get angry.

I know, I know, you're the hero of your story, and if every fairytale is true, only villains get angry, right?

But let's look at some other things that happen in cartoons that don't happen in real life:

- Pumpkins turn into beautiful carriages to take you to the ball.
- Little birdies help you get dressed in the morning.
- Mops and brooms operate themselves to clean your house.
- Animals talk, with real human voices, and they all understand each other.
- Mermaids have perfect hair under water.

I think you can see where I'm going with this.

Movies and cartoons are not fact, not science, not investigative journalism. It is perfectly okay to watch these things happen in fictional universes and not believe them to be universal truth in this reality. Instead, why don't we look at some real world expressions of sacred anger that we can use as examples of what is possible.

Martin Luther King Jr.
During the American Civil Rights movement, Martin Luther King Jr., a minister and activist used his anger at the injustices and inequalities

that black people were experiencing to be a loud and active voice that propelled a lot of change in a generation resisting it. He went on to win the Nobel Peace Prize.

Nelson Mandela
Revolutionary-turned-political leader, Nelson Mandela rose into the public eye during his resistance to apartheid, resulting in him spending 27 years in prison. He became the country's first Black head of state, and committed to uniting South Africa and racial reconciliation. His legacy is one of peace, justice, and intelligence.

Malala Yousafzai
Having fewer rights than her male peers in Pakistan simply for her gender made Malala Yousafzai become an activist at a young age. She denied intimidation by the Taliban who wanted to silence her for advocating for education for herself and her female peers, and survived a gunshot to the head when she persisted. She's the youngest Nobel Prize Winner, and today she's continuing her work to advocate for women and girls.

Greta Thunberg
Once you see and feel a need for change, it's

hard not to do something about it. In the case of Greta Thunberg, the need for change was how we are treating the environment. She didn't allow the fact that others might dismiss her for being neurodiverse and a child stop her unwavering pursuit.

Greta became a voice for the environmental movement, travelling the world, putting her outrage to work at rallies and protests. She took a lot of heat on social media, people criticizing a lot more than her age, and she didn't let it stop her, because her commitment to the movement was greater than anything else. When you hear her speak, you can feel her palpable fear of the direction we're taking the planet, but also the hope that something different is possible if we're willing to work together for change. She is a force to be reckoned with.

Traditions of Anger

As with changing anything in life, it's easy to fall back to the default setting. "That's always the way it's been" or "It is how it is" are probably the biggest killers of change in our lives . We can't stop innovating, growing, learning, trying... stagnation is death. To put it bluntly: just because that's the way it's always been, doesn't mean you can't choose to do it differently.

There comes a time where we need to put the comfort of our familiar status quo (even though it's unhealthy, hurtful, and in many ways, uncomfortable af) to the side, and be willing to experience the growing pains that come from trying something new. Once we become adults, we don't get to blame our upbringing for our actions. The things that have happened may not have been our fault, but working through it is our responsibility. Particularly if we want to actively choose how we engage with life, instead of always reacting from a place of trauma. If we don't like something, we need to change it.

I realize what I'm saying is hard - I don't want to downplay that, or tell you that it's as simple as snapping your fingers and voila - instant change. When we grow up around unhealthy expressions of anger, it's easy to create a story around it. Either we create our own unhealthy expressions of anger and blame it on how we were raised, or we repress our anger so far, denying its existence, because we're trying not to play out everything we witnessed as kids.

Neither of these will work.

When we start to take personal responsibility for our feelings and our actions, we become empowered to create a life on our terms - not on the default factory setting we were given in our DNA and the environments we grew up in. And while it may not be easy to undo all that programming, it is possible. Especially with the right support team in place.

It's easier to bury it than deal with it.

Cost/benefit analysis is a constant in life, and dealing with your anger is no exception. Typically we consider just the dollars and cents of the situation. What I've learned is that the energetic cost should also be factored in.

If you compare the costs of maintaining the status quo ($0) with getting to the root of how you feel ($$$) it seems like a no-brainer. What you'll find, though, is that the energy and money you save is a false economy.

Let's look at the math...

If you start dealing with the underlying issues that are causing you to be angry in therapy, and you're paying $200 for a session, and you go twice a month, you know the exact cost of dealing with your shit. It's $400 a month, or $4800 a year. It's a sure thing – there are no hypotheticals here. And compared to the $0 of not working through your problems, that looks like a pretty hefty investment.

But look a little closer.

What are the health costs associated with your anger? Do you have blood pressure medication? Antidepressants or tranquilizers? What about the time off work?

What are the emotional costs associated with your anger? Have you lost partners? Is your household tense where everyone walks on pins and needles? Are you experiencing real happiness? Do people like you? Do you like you?

Suddenly that $4800 isn't looking so bad, right?

It isn't always about the money though. As an example, sometimes expressing to a partner that you're unhappy will go predictably badly because they're not receptive to that sort of feedback, so you think it's easier to bury it (with no explicitly known consequence) than deal with it (when you know it'll upset them). This becomes a case of "Better the devil you know than the devil you don't." But in doing that, in denying how you feel, you are betraying yourself. You aren't honouring your truth, and you're settling for less than you deserve because you weren't willing to take a stand for the wonderfulness that is you. And that's not ideal.

We need to get comfortable with the uncomfortable if we want to move and grow, whether it's our own discomfort, or that of the people around us when we step into our truths. It's the only way to make any real, long lasting change. And you are 100% worth every dang bit.

SACRED SOUL SEARCHING

Here are the reflection questions to take to your journal:

What beliefs do I have about anger that make it hard for me to feel or talk about it?

Who are examples (in my life or in the media) that prove those beliefs to be untrue?

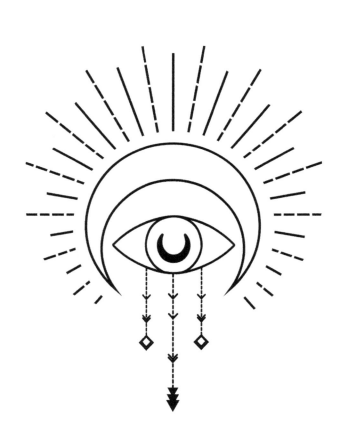

CHAPTER 3
Why anger gets a bad rap

When I was a kid anger was something that I saw expressed frequently, but never in a healthy, safe way. To be honest, I'm having a hard time narrowing it down to just one story to illustrate why we feel so unsafe around other people's anger because there were so many.

When I was 11, I befriended a boy in the neighbourhood named Jeff. He was older than me by a few years but shared my childlike innocence. He had a love for airplanes, and we'd sit under the big sky listening to them go by, and he'd tell me which ones were overhead. Or at least he told me that he was - I knew nothing about airplanes, so for all I knew it was a flying Toyota.

Jeff was blind. I'd had a blind babysitter before meeting him so this wasn't a novel thing, just one of the aspects of him that I had to factor in when we'd spend time together in the park behind our houses. We'd tell each other secrets, and laugh until the sun went down and it was time to go in for dinner. He was fun, and made me feel safe.

I'm not entirely sure why, but there was something about Jeff that my brother absolutely hated. Typically he'd make fun of him at the dinner table, and make fun of me for befriending him, but I'd heard worse and brushed it off. But one day he decided to direct his distaste for Jeff toward him directly and, shockingly, spat in his face. Jeff had no way to know it was escalating that far. He was given no reason. No warning. He wasn't able to dodge it, or fight back, and had the undignified experience of having to sit there and take it.

It was heartbreaking.

I ran home and told my dad what my brother had just done. This cruel, angry expression of contempt that was completely unprovoked. I remember wanting him to get into trouble, but I could never have anticipated what happened next.

My brother was in trouble a lot when we were kids, so witnessing him get yelled at was a pretty regular occurrence that I'd become desensitized to. But this was different. My dad yelled louder, and longer than I'd ever seen him yell before, and it culminated with my dad spitting in my brother's face.

Fire fought with fire.

I immediately regretted telling my dad. Not because him spitting at my brother in any way nullified the horrible thing that had been done to my friend, but because now my brother was also humiliated and treated like he was less than. And I believed it was all my fault.

Looking back with almost 30 years of distance, I can understand (but not agree with) how this whole thing went down. My dad had no idea how to cope with his kid being so blatantly rude to someone. My brother was prideful and stubborn, and no amount of yelling would make him repent, so my dad escalated. I'm sure he thought that if my brother experienced the same kind of indignity it would teach him some compassion, and some empathy, and this type of thing would never happen again. But that's not the kind of kid my brother was.

And then there was me. I felt responsible for Jeff because if we hadn't been hanging out, my brother would have had no reason to go after him. And if I hadn't tattled to my dad, my brother wouldn't have been spat at. Anger has a funny way of stretching itself out like a dudebro manspreading on the subway. Blame starts to float around and no one's held accountable. Except someone was accountable.

My brother was responsible for his actions. At 10 years old, he knew enough about the world that he understood that spitting in someone's face was a shitty thing to do. He may have been raised poorly, but if you know the difference between right or wrong, you can't go around blaming your childhood for your bad choices.

My dad was responsible for his actions. His inability to control the situation, his disappointment in my brother, the stress from his day, the traffic on the commute, his own shitty childhood, whatever. These are contributing factors, but the fact remains that he, the adult, chose to yell and spit at his 10 year old son. And that's no good.

Somehow, the two people who felt shittiest about this all were me and Jeff. My dad and brother walked around blaming everyone else for their actions instead of owning up to their stuff and actively choosing to do better next time.

Anger is unpredictable.

People fear anger because of its unpredictability. There is a sense of security that comes from knowing what's happening next, so when we throw anger into the mix, we lose that safety net. I sometimes joke that my training in improv theatre helped me navigate the anger I experienced in my childhood, but there's actually a bit of truth to that. When we're in a tense situation, and our nervous systems shifts into fight or flight, we are ready for anything. It's the physical equivalent of the "Yes, and..." prompts that comes from performing improv. You don't know what's coming, but you're poised and ready for whatever happens next. You need to be quick on your toes, whether it's to diffuse a situation with words, or to run like hell because your safety is no longer a guarantee.

But what happens when that unpredictability isn't in others but within ourselves? It's one thing to find someone else's anger uncomfortable, we can always get up and leave, but when it's bubbling beneath our own chest there isn't much space to run.

The fighter within

Inside me, there lives this little aspect of myself that is always ready to fight, she's like my inner Ruth Langmore. (If you haven't seen the TV show Ozark, Ruth is a foul-mouthed, fiercely-loyal, rough-around-the-edges kinda gal.) If I trace back her origin she's probably me at about 13 years old, tired of living a life that felt scary all the damn time. My home life was a mess. My dad's drunken explosions eventually became too much, causing me to move out. I moved in with my mom in a neighbourhood with a high crime rate and fear so thick in the air you could feel it even if you weren't an Empath. We lived in city housing, so I was surrounded by lack and poverty. There was always fear everything would be taken away, or that my physical safety was a risk because I was a young woman who walked alone at night. A lot. I was a great student at school, class president, but I was being threatened by a female classmate and I was regularly fondled by my male classmates because I'd developed breasts before the other girls. Change didn't happen, no matter how many times I reported it to my teachers.

There wasn't one place at that point in time that felt safe to me.

I had a lot to be angry about, and even though it feels like a lifetime ago, the inner Ruth in me feels it like it was yesterday. When I started high school, in a new neighbourhood, where nobody knew my story, I thought I'd see the end of her. Sure, I got angry, but I tried to keep it contained. I dabbled more in the fear in those years, with the tension at home, and the risks of being a woman, and being worried I'd be 'outed' at school as having come from poverty. The anger didn't have as much place to be present, or at the very least the fear was a convincing mask. It wasn't until my mid 30s when I started doing a lot of shadow work that the Inner Ruth began showing up. Which was a bit surprising to be honest, because I'd really felt like after lots of counselling and 10 years of inner work that I was #overit.

Whenever Ruth would show up, I've got to be honest, it would scare the living shit out of me. To feel that out of alignment with my usual "love and light" nature, to tap into this primal, dark side of myself and to feel the weight of it, of her, and to have what feels like zero control when it would happen... it was not with the happy making. I remember this one event a couple of years ago, that I'm really not proud of, where I'd completely snapped. The only thing I can remember is shouting at my computer, "I'm going to kill this bitch." Over and over and over again. (Like enough times that I'm surprised my neighbours didn't call the police – especially if they didn't know I wasn't speaking literally.) Once I made it to the other side of that anger I felt raw, exhausted, and emotionally spent. It was like I'd survived this horrific event that was all a blur, and I had no idea what had happened.

Aside from the fear of "Shit, what's she going to do next?" which is actually quite similar to how I'd feel with other people's anger, there was also a cocktail of other feelings. Guilt and regret about whatever I'd said and did when Ruth was at the wheel. Shame about not being over it, and the fact that there was still that much anger within me, even after over a decade of deep inner work and healing.

But what if it didn't have to be that way?

Spoiler alert: it doesn't.

Calling out anger

Did you ever have a time when you were a kid, trying to fall asleep in your dark room but the shadows were there, looking really ominous and taunting you? "Go ahead and sleep... wait 'til you see the nightmares I have in store for you." They'd whisper. And sometimes you would – sheer exhaustion would make you fall asleep, and sometimes, the nightmares did come. But other times you'd be like "Fuck that shadows!", hop out of bed, turn on the lights and see that there was nothing to be afraid of in the first place? Anger is a lot like that.

When it goes unexamined we get to mythologize it. Anger becomes this big, scary, daunting thing that we couldn't possibly overcome. And so we close our eyes and pretend it isn't there. We force ourselves to fall asleep so we can just carry on. When really all we need to do is turn on the damn lights, see it for what it really is, and stop letting the fear of it control us.

When we view anger as sacred, we stop resisting it and we allow it to move through us. The resistance is where the trouble lies – it's what brings in the lack of control, it's what expresses all the hurtful things we wouldn't otherwise say, it's what brings the guilt, the regret, and the shame. All of this is unnecessary. If we make it a regular practice to say what we think and to honour our feelings, there's nothing that's repressed and buried that needs to sneak out when anger gives it an opportunity. If we make a habit of expressing our anger as it comes up, instead of burying it down and then exploding, there's a lot less ammunition when the explosion does happen. Which makes it a lot less scary, a lot more controlled, and by extension, a lot more predictable. When we stop making anger the villain of the piece, we're able to use it as a compass to show us what aspects we still have left to heal. Anger is a sacred teacher, but we need to have the courage and the willingness to listen to it.

SACRED SOUL SEARCHING

Here are the reflection questions to take to your journal:

What is it I fear most about the potential of my anger?

What would be the best possible outcome for my life, if my anger was healthily expressed?

Part 2
Understanding Anger

CHAPTER 4

You're not angry, you're feeling something else entirely

In a world telling you who to be, what to buy, and how to act, it would be pretty unfair of me to tell you how you're feeling. You've gotten this far, you're a grown ass person who has been feeling things since you've entered the world. So consider this chapter an invitation to get curious...

Here's the thing with anger: things are rarely as they appear. So we can't decide that what we are experiencing on the surface is the truth, the whole truth, and nothing but the truth.

When we view things from a place of curiosity, we shift the ingrained beliefs we have when we've declared something to be true. We allow ourselves to explore what's possible, knowing that we may not be right. (And what a gift to be open to the possibility of not being right! Pressure OFF!)

As someone who has lived a pretty tumultuous life and has ridden the emotional roller coaster so long that I no longer get queasy on the dips, here is what I know to be true:

Anger is easier to experience than a lot of other feelings.

Even when we fear it. Even when it's uncomfortable. Even when it's unpredictable.

Because as awful as anger can be to experience, it feels a lot safer to us than some other emotions. Especially if it's been our default setting since childhood. Anger is the mask we wear, oftentimes unconsciously, because it feels a lot less vulnerable than some other raw emotions that are playing out beneath the surface.

So with that in mind, let's take a look at some of the usual suspects who are actually pulling the strings when we think we're fully embodying anger.

You're not angry, you're sad.

This is one of the most common experiences I've seen in people. For men, they're raised to not feel emotions, and certainly not cry, so anger becomes a convenient mask that protects their masculinity (because somewhere, at some time, people decided that anger was a masculine emotion...) For women, we're raised to believe that we're too sensitive and feel things too deeply, so anger allows us to hide those feelings we'd be judged for, and deny how we actually feel so we don't have to deal with it. For those who are gender non-conforming, they feel the weight of both of these experiences.

Aside from the external conditioning that may make us want to mask our feelings, we have all the internal stuff playing out as well. When we examine sadness, it becomes a lot to unpack. It results in some honest but awkward conversations with yourself about the things going on in your life that may need to change in order for you to be happy. And that's uncomfortable AF. If you're unwilling to make those changes the sadness starts to spiral into other things like hopelessness, overwhelm, or depression. It's a lot, so one can easily see why it would be easier to get some of that energy moving, using anger as the tool to make it happen. Let's give you a bit of grace for when this happens - your tender heart needs it.

You're not angry, you're scared.

There is nothing quite like fear to make you feel small and powerless. And isn't the whole benefit of being an adult (which comes with all the drawbacks like bills, taxes, and grey hairs) that you get to finally start being in control of your life?

Yes. Unless fear decides to jump in the driver's seat and you get stuck riding shotgun.

The thing with the feelings of powerlessness that fear creates is that it reverts us back to our youngest selves. We often forget the tools we've cultivated for this very purpose and find ourselves transfixed, deers in headlights, unable to make a move. And if we give into that fear that freeze response is all consuming, so nothing gets done.

Well, anger has the opposite response.

Anger is fuel - it has a knack for moving us forward and taking action (any action!) because it's so uncomfortable burning inside of us otherwise. So if fear is passive and something happening to us, anger is active - or more accurately REACTIVE - and it shifts the dynamic to us doing something.

It's easy to imagine that if in your normal life you're someone who feels pretty capable and responsible, when that debilitating freeze response creeps in you'll want to feel anything but. Oftentimes we don't even realize that anger is the mask for fear because, honestly, feeling powerless is something to get angry about. It takes a little digging and a willingness to be wrong to see beyond the initial response and acknowledge what lies beneath. And then to sit with that - it's not fun, and requires some deep compassion with yourself when you've cultivated the courage to dig in.

You're not angry, you're disappointed.

There is a beautiful child-like innocence that we allow ourselves to have when we believe. Whether it's spoken or unspoken expectations, or just having faith in someone or something outside of ourselves, being able to suspend cynicism or disbelief is a really beautiful thing.

Until things don't pan out.

Allowing ourselves to believe taps into the inner child, which is the sweetest part of ourselves.

Naturally, the impulse would be to react from that space, but a child-like state comes with a full spectrum of emotions - not just that sweetness. . Everything we've been taught about what it means to be an adult says that you can't just lash out in a childish tantrum, so we bury down that immediate heart-burning sensation of disappointment and cover it up with being righteously pissed off - because somehow that's more adult.

The irony of this is that when we look at the unhealthy ways this type of anger is expressed: yelling, punching holes in the walls, saying hurtful things - they are all rooted in that same impulsivity we have as kids, before we learned that there's a certain conduct that's expected of us as citizens of this planet. In this case not only is anger not the immediate feeling we're experiencing, but we've convinced ourselves that we're dealing with it. When, in reality, the smallest parts of ourselves are sitting in disappointment about whatever let them down and then the rejection of not being fully seen, heard, and expressed.

You're not angry, you're feeling rejected.

I grew up around a lot of families with three

kids, and this always created a curious dynamic between them. The expression "three's a crowd" always played out – they'd always group off in two to one, and usually there was one kid who was always part of the duo. So what happens to the third kid, in particular when it's always the same two who partner off?

A lot of times they get pretty angry. And rightfully so.

When we're cast out, especially when we don't know why, it creates a lot of feelings within that may not have been there otherwise. We start to ask ourselves questions like:

Why don't they like me?
Did I do something to upset them?
What's wrong with me?

Suddenly we've totally internalized the actions of others to produce a distorted reflection of ourselves. And let's be honest – it's not just kids who do this. This dynamic lasts well beyond the playground and high school. Think about when you weren't invited to a wedding that your friends were. Or you were passed up for a promotion. Or the person who you've been into for ages has kept you solidly in the friend zone. Somehow we start convincing ourselves that there's something wrong with us, rather than it just being a misalignment, or people were busy, or just preferred the company of others.

But do we actually want to admit that to ourselves?

Hell no!

It's way easier to create a story about how shitty we are and why someone else was better because it keeps us from shining too brightly (and thus outshining the other people around us). It keeps us fitting in, not rocking the boat, and maintaining the status quo. Now perhaps "easier" isn't as appropriate a word as "convenient" because there is nothing particularly easy about thinking shit about yourself, but not having the discomfort of stretching and growing does have a certain degree of comfort to it.

But where does anger come into all of that?

We resent the discomfort that comes from those uncomfortable questions. We hate what they bring up. We have this little voice in our heads that whispers a lot of nasty stuff in our ear, so when we feel rejected, it's like that voice gets confirmation that it was right - that we are terrible people, and the little voice happy-dances all over our insides.

Who wouldn't get pissed off about that?

But if we just swim in the anger, if we don't dive deep and see what's underneath, then we're not addressing the hurt of the rejection, or the fact that there's a part of us that feels unworthy and unlovable in the first place. When we leave these aspects unresolved, it leaves us open to repeating the cycle with more hurt, more shitty feelings, more resentment. And then the anger that masks all of it, when we could just turn the spotlight on the initial hurt and focus our efforts on healing that instead.

You're not angry, you're feeling shame, guilt, or regret.

Here's an interesting peek behind the curtain: at the time of writing this, I'm feeling pretty guilty. I asked my husband, who inspired this section, if I could mention him in my book, but instead of asking delicately, I launched in with, "You know how the only time you're an asshole is because you're feeling shame. Can I write about that?" Unsurprisingly, the answer was no, and it's been over an hour of awkward silence, even after I apologized.

There was a time when I'd have gotten really defensive about this and blamed him for the guilt and regret I'm currently feeling, which would have left me rather haughty and self righteous. But instead, I'm taking my lumps. I've apologized and I'm giving him time to come around... because sometimes when someone walks over and just rips off your bandaid without any warning, you need a little time.

So how did I get to this place of being willing to sit in the discomfort I caused instead of being angry about it? (I'd like it on record that I'm resisting making a joke about being raised Catholic and how familiar it is to feel shame as a form of penance.)

I recognized a few things:

- Regardless of my intentions, my actions have consequences and I need to live with them.

- My husband's hurt is entirely valid, and

being angry about it would be completely unfair to him.

- Taking personal responsibility for my actions is one of my governing forces (likely because it's one I had to work hard to learn outside of my upbringing), so it's important for my integrity to own up to what I did.

Is there a part of me that's feeling a bit sanctimonious and wants to say, "Well, if the truth hurts…" or "Well, you do do that…"? Yes, but that would do a lot more harm than good.

Plus, it kinda worked out to be a wonderful illustration for this chapter, so it's not all bad.

Deflecting with anger when we feel something uncomfortable (and is there anything less comfortable than shame?) is so much easier than the work I did above. And when we can spin our shame into shaming someone else, then the burden feels a bit lighter, and they're less likely to bring it up because they're feeling pretty shitty themselves. It becomes a tool, sure, but not a healthy one. So instead of using it to move the energy through you, it becomes more like a bunch of monkeys flinging their poop. Everyone gets dirty, and no one has any fun.

So if anger is such a convincing mask, how can you tell when it's real?

I'm not saying that anger is an illusion and that it's always a mask for something else. Sometimes anger is just anger. But that doesn't mean we have to take it at face value. It does us no harm to have some curiosity about our anger and to examine if it's how we truly feel. Because here's the thing: when we use anger as a mask for all of this and more, we don't actually get to the heart of what's bothering us. We aren't dealing with the underlying root cause so not only does that emotion still sit there, marinating, we also keep putting on the anger mask to avoid dealing with it. It can start happening so seamlessly that we forget these are emotions, and not who we actually are.

Living life in anger doesn't just feel unpleasant (even if it's keeping you protected from all those other feelings), it's also really hard on your nervous system and it's a denial of the other emotions underneath. As soon as we start shoving things down and burying them away, we start to create other problems - not just with ourselves and our psyches, but in our work and our relationships with the people around us. Feelings were meant to be expressed, and it's hard to do that if you're unable to acknowledge them for what they are.

So your invitation is this... when you feel the anger start to rise, take a moment to check in about what's actually driving anger to the surface. Do it with zero expectations or judgment - just an open state of curiosity, because the purpose is to get you to reflect and grow, not shame and blame yourself into silence. Don't forget: if you need some questions to get you started, don't forget to download the virtual journal at sacredangerbook.com.

SACRED SOUL SEARCHING

Here are the reflection questions to take
to your journal:

*I feel this anger. What else am I feeling?
(Name it to claim it.)*

*What can I learn about all the things I'm
feeling in this moment?*

CHAPTER 5
Owning your anger
+ making a plan

It's time for a moment of tough love...

Personal responsibility is probably the biggest piece to the happiness puzzle, but it's the one that makes people the most uncomfortable. This next section will be chock full of tough love, but I need you to see it through, m'kay? Take as many breaks as you need - there is medicine in this for you.

What if I told you that YOU were ultimately the reason for your anger? You'd think I was a jerk, right? Here's what I'd like you to know right out of the gate.

I'm okay with you not liking me if it means you will ask yourself the tough, but necessary questions that will help you own up to your stuff. My job (with my clients, my podcast, and even here with this book) is to create the space for you to have some raw, honest conversations with yourself. Some of it might be uncomfortable. Much of it is likely things you haven't been willing to look at before. And that's okay. Because you're here now, and we're in this together.

So let me circle back...

You, yes YOU are the reason for your anger.

It's not your shitty boss, the barista who screwed up your nonfat soy vanilla latte with extra foam, or Brenda on the PTA, even though those things can be pretty frustrating. It's not your husband's inability to unload the dishwasher, or the dance recitals and soccer practice you need to rush your kids to. It's not the economy, or world politics, or the environment. It's not the traffic on your long commute, your computer crashing, or Mercury being in retrograde. (That poor planet gets blamed for everything.)

It's you.

Now let me tell you why that's a good thing.

When we're busy looking outside for things to

feel good, we're always going to be left wanting. There will always be something going on to distract from our happiness, or to make us spiral into shame or regret. Happiness is an inside job, and when we take personal responsibility, we're able to make the changes that'll help us feel, well, better. Suddenly we're back in the driver's seat of our lives, the heroine of our own stories. We have the power of choice. When we own up to it, we claim our ability to choose differently. And that my friend, is power.

We've all been dealt different hands, and society certainly favours some people considerably more than others. But at the end of the day, the cards in your hand are the ones you have to play. So what's your move?

Here's the thing: we're uncomfortable with personal responsibility. It's easier to get angry and blame everyone else than to look at the role we played in the very things we're pissed off about. And everything outside of us that's saying "you just need to remain high vibe" or "love and light" when inside you're feeling "fuck love and light – I'm IN IT right now" is really doing us a disservice. We need to give ourselves permission to feel exactly what we're feeling, not pretending this aspect of the self isn't there.

This is not the time to ostrich, folks. Head out of the sand, tout de suite.

The spiritual community has done a great job of validating our good emotions, but as a whole, it has denied any aspect of shadow work, which only half of the work we do as lightworkers. It's impossible to remain in the light (and in integrity) while denying the darkness within us. We all have it, it's part of the human experience. And when we try to normalize the "love and light" way of being, we diminish our darker times and we deny ourselves the lessons they hold. And that's not spiritual work my friend, it's spiritual bypassing.

We not only need to get comfortable with our own anger but with the anger of others. (Though it's perfectly okay, and encouraged to have some boundaries about what you're willing to allow.) There is medicine in that discomfort. Most times, people don't need us to solve their problems, they just want to be seen and heard, and have their feelings validated. They're battling their own feelings about wanting to resist the anger, feeling unsafe to express their most primal selves, and they need to know they're okay and not wrong for feeling everything that's coming up for them. And if we don't have the right words, we just need to create some space to be held, so they can go through whatever they're going through without feeling encumbered. (And likewise, we need to ask those around us to create this space when we're deeply in it too.)

It sounds simple, but one of the best things you can do is ask, "What do you need right now?" If they just want to vent, let them vent. If they want to problem solve, you can help with that too. But taking that brief pause to make sure you're showing up in a way that's actually helpful can really make all the difference. It does however ask us to be secure with where we're at, in order to hold that space, particularly for someone else's anger. It can be hard to say, "I don't have the emotional bandwidth for this right now." especially if you're a recovering people pleaser like me, but it honestly does so much less damage than trying to help (notice I said 'trying') when you're not in the right headspace to do so.

If you identify as an empath or a highly sensitive person, this becomes an even bigger task, because not only are you dealing with what's being said, and holding space for it, but you're also FEELING IT ALL, including whatever it brings up within you. You'll want to make sure you've got some solid grounding in place, and some energy clearing tools at hand to help you afterward. (Make sure to check out the advice in Chapter 9 to help get you through.)

Back to our OWN anger...

When we don't accept what we're feeling because it's not the right time (is there ever a right time?), because it doesn't feel safe, because it isn't "nice", or because it makes ourselves or someone else uncomfortable, we start to break down. We create these fragments of ourselves, each of these moments when we've denied our feelings (but especially when that feeling is anger), where a part of us has splintered off. It starts from a very young age, and then we hit adulthood and we're wondering why we feel broken. In some types of shamanism they consider this to be soul fragmentation, and people can journey back to these moments where they rejected a piece of themself, so they can perform a soul retrieval in order to restore a feeling of wholeness, on a soul level.

We are whole and complete, but we've been casting out these aspects of ourselves for so long that it feels normal. We've forgotten our wholeness. We need to work on identifying the parts of us that have been lost, healing the feelings attached to them, and then re-integrating them into the people we are today, so we can feel that wholeness we crave. The way to do that is by stopping the denial of our uncomfortable feelings. But what does that even look like?

Accepting ourselves - our messy selves and our most glamorous selves - as whole and complete is the most radical act of self love you can make. There is a bajillion dollar industry, several of them in fact, that want to convince you there's something wrong with you in order to sell you something you probably don't need. There's a quick fix and a magic pill for basically every one of life's problems. In the case of anger, it's likely pharmaceutical. If you can look yourself in the eye in the mirror and say, "You know what, this is a bad hair day. I'm a good person. I express how I feel. I'm proud of my impact in the world. And that makes it all okay." then you're winning at the game of life.

It's possible to identify things you may not like

about yourself (including emotions like anger, or the behaviours that come out of it) and still like yourself as a whole being. It's not black and white. Humans are complex creatures, and multifaceted - we can't expect ourselves to be one way all of the time. Claiming these aspects of ourselves is a big part of taking responsibility - and it's where change begins.

So... you've taken a look at the things you're not happy with, you've accepted responsibility for the ways you've contributed to this, but how angry are you really?

Because let's be honest: there's a lot of stuff to be angry about in the world, especially right now. There's white supremacy, politics, sexual assault, the patriarchy, police brutality, animal cruelty, and abuse. There's inequality with race, gender, sexual orientation and social status. There is JUST SO MUCH.

But here's the thing, love: getting riled up by your Facebook page or Twitter feed, or by reading the news and blowing up the comment section isn't going to help anyone (except perhaps the makers of your favourite Antacid) if you aren't going to do anything about it. You're encouraged to feel all the feels, but also: you've got a finite amount of energy, so I also suggest you pick your battles. Does this mean you stop caring about all the other injustices in the world because the thing that lights the biggest fire in your belly is the Black Lives Matter movement? Hell no. It does mean you may need to get some blinders on so you don't develop an ulcer from scrolling social media on your sofa. Here are some ways to keep you focused, without needing to become a hermit in the woods with zero access to wifi:

Limit how much news you watch and read.

My first studies in college were in broadcast communications, and in the newsroom we had this term "If it bleeds, it leads". Fear and shock (two things that can make you angry) are the biggest tactics to getting your attention. And because of the instant gratification of the online news cycle, the race to break the story first (and get the most clicks for advertisers) is such that they manipulate information and create click-baity headlines in order to get your attention. And of course once you're on their site, they've got several other headlines that get your attention and get you angry, and down the rabbit hole you go. (Plus now you're pissed off about stuff you didn't care that much about in the first place.) Find a couple of legitimate news sources, and check in on them every few days. Stick to the highlights. If anything major is happening that needs your attention, you can be dang sure someone will be ranting about it on social media.

Speaking of social media... watch who and what you follow.

Engagement is the language of the algorithm. So when you're clicking and commenting on posts that upset you (because let's be honest: social media gives us a voice that just wasn't available to us only a decade ago) they will keep showing you content that upsets you. And if your goal is to be angry all the time then that's the way to do it. But if you want a healthy balance so you're free to express all the emotions that come up for you, then you'll want to diversify the content you engage with and the people you follow. (Plus this will help your feed fill back up with cute babies and animal stories from the friends on your feed, which definitely give you the warm and fuzzy feels.)

Vote with your dollars, your time, your voice.

If the plot of "You've Got Mail" breaks your heart

(a small independant neighbourhood book store is chewed up by a big box book chain), spend your money on small, independent businesses. If you're upset about the tragedies people of colour face, share your platform with them, share their stories on social media, invest in their businesses, learn from them, and use your privilege to call in your friends and family who maybe haven't worked out that it's not "all lives matter". If you're fed up of seeing people discriminated against for their gender or sexuality, show up as an ally, speak up when you hear hate speech, go to the parades, vote for the candidates that believe in these causes (and show it with their actions, not just their words.) Be a safe space. And in every case, find the charities that are doing the work against the things that make you angry and give them your money. If you don't have money to spare, volunteer your time or spread their content. Help in any way you can.

Are you consciously ready to make the necessary changes so you can stop being so angry?

While being angry may be uncomfortable AF, sometimes it's a lot easier than having an honest conversation with yourself about what needs to shift and then putting those shifts into action. I get it. When I was in corporate, I desperately wanted to leave and could feel my soul withering with each day spent in my cubicle. Then, my grandpa became terminally ill, and I spent his last two weeks visiting him across the country. I'd sit and hold his hand until the little red light on my blackberry would start blinking. I'd excuse myself, answer some emails, sell some software, then head back to his bedside. With the benefit of hindsight, I want to ask my 28 year old self "Are you for-fucking-real?"

After he passed and I could reflect on how I'd spent those two weeks, I could see how disconnected my priorities were from how I spent my time, and I knew I needed to make a change. But the knowing wasn't enough: I hadn't yet built up the courage to make the leap. It wasn't until the 2008 recession was fully experienced in Canada (mid 2009) and I was laid off that I left that job. And was it because I loved the work, or enjoyed the committed relationship I was in with my blackberry? Hell no. It's probably also worth noting that the owner of my company had nicknamed me Little Ball of Rage - so I wasn't the only one who knew I was miserable.

But here are the uncomfortable truths:

- I had zero confidence in myself, or the value I brought. I knew my radio degree wasn't going to cut it, and I wasn't convinced I was a good enough marketer to offer my skills to anyone paying what I currently made. (Especially in an economic downturn.)

- I wanted to work for a worthy cause like a nonprofit, but they're not known for their paycheques. I was making damn good money in corporate, with quarterly bonuses, and my salary would be cut in half. The reality is that while money may not buy happiness, it does keep food in your mouth and a roof over your head, and I was raising my teenage sister at the time.

- I was afraid. What if I'd made this earth-shattering decision (at least that's how it felt at the time) and I still felt empty and worthless after, but with less money? I could also hear one of my colleague's voices saying "Better the devil you know than the devil you don't." so I stayed put.

Am I proud of this? Naw. I basically just told you that I wanted to live this big, bold life, but I was way too chicken to go after it. The harsh truth is that until change was forced on me, I was holding onto what was uncomfortably comfortable and familiar.

Sometimes we need to do what's comfortable. It's all our nervous system can take. Even if what's comfortable feels awfully terrible. The light walker's journey is not for everyone – in fact, all of this was happening at the very start of my journey, so I hadn't built up the faith to get me through those dark times. So love, if you're still in the chapter where you're stuck in the muck, you'll receive zero judgment from me.

But when you're ready – the world better watch out.

There's a Chinese proverb that says, "When sleeping women wake, mountains move." This is the potential you tap into when you're ready to say "Enough is enough."

But how do you know when you've reached that point? Here's a few tell-tale signs:

- You are way more irritated than you used to be. Even the smallest thing sets you off.
- "Fuck this shit" becomes your personal mantra.
- Your blood pressure is rising, or you're having new stomach trouble.
- You get tension headaches, and sore shoulders – like you're literally carrying the weight of the world with you.
- You keep hearing yourself say "I can't do this anymore."

So now that you've acknowledged you're ready to make some changes, it's time to uncover exactly what's pissing you off so you can come up with a plan of what you can do about it. Here's an exercise you can try:

Step 1: Take Stock
Start making a list of all the things going on in your life and how they make you feel. Are they helping you, or hindering you? If you feel them in your body, do you feel open and expansive, or do you contract and close down? We're being curious in this process, not judging it.

Step 2: Evaluate Your List
For the things that feel really good you can

draw a little heart beside them, and take a moment to be grateful they're in your life. For everything else, we need a new list.

Step 3: Categorise The Shit.
Create a table with these three headings: Needs a Plan, Delegate Elsewhere, Let It Go. Take the items that feel really icky from your first list and put them under the category they belong to. If it's something you can let go (like being annoyed by your neighbour not mowing their lawn), put it under that heading and when you feel yourself getting riled up about it remind yourself that, for the sake of your health, you're letting it go.

For the items you've marked to be delegated (like being stressed out because you need to hire help at home or at work), decide who will be dealing with it, and when you want it done by. The items under Needs a Plan will be your biggest undertaking, because it's the stuff that affects you most, and you can't get help with. This is where you'll want to decide how to invest your energy – whether it's in education, activism, making courageous leaps, and so on. Again, you'll want to write down what the plan is, and when you want to do it by. The more specific you can be, the better. (Studies show you're 42% more likely to achieve a goal if you write it down.)

Don't forget: it's okay to ask for help.

Somehow we bought into this story that we have to do it alone. Yeah, it's great to be strong, capable and independent, but if it's costing you the ability to get out of a rut then you're doing yourself zero favours. Help takes so many different forms, and it really depends on what sort of struggle you're feeling yourself in. For me, help has looked like therapy, herbal and floral remedies (as well as antidepressants), coaches, energetic and body work and a ton of spiritual exploration and mentorship. For others, it's a personal trainer and exercise, it's a nutritionist, it's guided meditations, it's chiro or acupuncture, or a physician. As they say, "No (wo)man is an island."

When I decided to hire my coach I'd been in a big funk for probably 4 months. It went from something that I thought would quickly pass to becoming my new way of life, and I was not digging it. It was having an impact on my marriage, my ability to parent, and my business. I just felt this cloud of "meh" hanging over me, no matter what I did. The exact words out of my mouth to her were, "I'm sick and tired of feeling like a piece of shit every day." and her response to me was perfect, "That's great. Tomorrow, you'll wake up and choose not to feel like a piece of shit." Sounds simple, right? But it kind of was.

All of that's true, but it didn't change the reality of the situation. I knew I needed help, but I was stuck in the stories and excuses that were holding me there. The impact of feeling so angry and so low had negatively impacted my business. I didn't have the full amount to invest, and hiring her would be the biggest investment I'd made in myself and my business. Putting up the money I did have, and committing to the rest was this powerful declaration that I was DONE with feeling that way. Fed up and ready for something new. And I was willing to bet on it. I was willing to bet on ME.

You've got to find the thing that works for you, and with the budget you have available to you so that you can begin doing the work to pull yourself out of this space that I lovingly refer to as "the shits". Because if you're really done with feeling shitty, like actually FED UP, then you need to back it with some action to make some change. Otherwise, you're just running all that anger onto a hamster wheel - and once you realize you're not going anywhere, it's going to feel a whole lot worse. When you decide that regardless of what's happening around you that YOU are in the driver's seat, it makes a world of difference.

"But when I was a kid/teenager/young adult ....happened."

The purpose of this chapter isn't to convince you that you don't have a reason to be pissed - your feelings are 100% valid. When you were hurt, shamed, made to feel unsafe, bullied and picked on, treated unfairly - all of that fucking sucks. Especially when the person or people doing it are your parents and those closest to you who should've been making you feel loved, cherished and safe above all else. (I recognize this is a lot of shorthand - please don't feel like I'm diminishing your pain here.)

Here is the part where the tough love comes in, my sweet:

There comes a time, especially when we are adults, where we need to accept that it's no longer our parents job to parent us, and we need to take care of that for ourselves. If we've got unresolved childhood trauma (I almost laughed typing "if" - of course we do!) then we can't wait for our parents to miraculously fix it - it's officially our problem to solve. We get to become the parents we needed, and we bestow that love, time and attention on our inner child. Some of this is work you do on your own - exploring, reflecting, meditating... looking at where the hurt still lives and shining the light in those parts. But a lot of this is work you do with a professional who can take you deeper than you can get on your own, and help you start stitching up any remnants of a wound you may have.

I have a good friend who was abused as a child by a family friend. Even though her parents didn't know it had happened, the hurt parts of her felt they should have, and even as an adult, she not only resented them, but had expectations that they owed her for what had happened (unspoken expectations at that). She knew it wasn't healthy, for herself or her relationship with them, but there was that hurt part of her that was stuck in the blame game: she was hurt, someone had to pay.

We talked about this a fair amount and actually had the tough love talk above: about how now that she's in her 40s she needs to stop expecting her parents to protect her from something that happened to her as a child. Especially with the adult knowledge that even if they could, it wasn't in their emotional skillset. (Because hey, it may suck, but parents are still human, and they're going to be flawed.) By taking ownership – not of what happened to her, but of the support she needed going forward – she was able to nurture the younger aspect of herself who had been holding onto the trauma for decades. And in many ways, her relationship with her parents shifted too, because she could love them as they are (instead of how she wished they were, or had been), and she stopped expecting them to make something right that was impossible to make right in the first place.

So when we come back to the statement from a few beats ago, "But when I was younger, ___ happened", my response would be (and I say it with the utmost love and respect): That really sucks. What are you going to do about it now?

So long as we stay attached to the stories of our past, part of us stays stuck there. It means we can't move forward, it means we stunt our own growth and our own success, and we're looking to someone else to fix it, when at the end of the day: we're the hero of the story and we get to choose what to do differently now that we're in the position to choose for ourselves.

Taking ownership of our anger stretches beyond us

When we take ownership of our lives, our anger, and our power, it doesn't just relate to the things that have been done to us in the past, but also how our actions affect those closest to us. This is where there's a bit of a fine line to walk, because it's important to be honest and honour your feelings – even when they're uncomfortable – but at the same time how you express those feelings has a consequence, and you need to own that too.

So how do you walk that line of being both honest and honouring of where you're at, while also being sincere when you're apologizing to your loved ones about how your feelings have impacted them?

You apologize for the actions you took, or the words you said that were hurtful, but not for the feelings behind them.

Because much like how your actions impacted how they feel, and those feelings are 100% valid, so too are the feelings you experienced that lead up to that moment. And it's not just anger. Since anger can be a mask for a myriad of other emotions, as you saw in chapter 4, it's important that your apology is validating your actual experience. Your feelings are just as valid as theirs and need to be included as part of the apology.

At the time of writing this I'm listening to some music from my youth. So, for a comical illustration, we're going to use the lyrics to the opening of The Barenaked Ladies song "One Week" to examine this some more.
Now, because of copyright issues I can't share them here, but they're easily found on Google. Mostly, I'm hoping it was catchy enough to still be in your head, all these years later.

He might start off with apologizing for whatever happened in the living room, for whatever was his fault, and for not telling her when he realized it, and for withholding the apology for an additional two days. But if he's just apologizing for his actions (and how they impacted her) then he's not actually talking about how he feels which is what contributed to the actions in the first place. He could share how it felt for her to laugh at him and dismiss him by telling him to get it together. By sharing openly, honestly, and apologetically, he's creating a space where she can talk about why she was angry in the first place, and anything else that contributed to the conflict.

The goal here is not to pretend the fight didn't happen, or that it doesn't hurt anymore, or to fill any sort of crater that's been left in the aftermath. The reason we do it this way is because it's how we begin to rebuild the bridges that anger burnt down. It's both sincere and apologetic, but also inclusive of our own pain and heartache so there's consensus - a meeting of the hearts and minds.

SACRED SOUL SEARCHING

Here are the reflection questions to take to your journal:

What are the top 3 things that bother me most right now (about my life, or the state of the world), and what about them am I feeling, specifically?

How would I like to feel instead, and what actions can I take to create a more positive outcome about those situations?

CHAPTER 6
Consequences of unexpressed/unmanaged anger

Talking about the consequences of not dealing with your anger can be a fine line between honesty and fear-mongering. It's the hardest truth you'll need to face about anger, so if you weren't convinced by now that something needs to change you will be after this chapter.

I wanted to make a distinction here between unexpressed anger and unmanaged anger because it's an essential part to this process; and, in many ways, the final step before you start the cycle all over again. Remember, this is not a destination we're arriving at, but a new way of being. This book isn't going to cure you of anger, the goal is to give you some tools so that it's not running your life.

Expressing your anger can be a really healthy way to deal with it, but only if you're backing it with action. There is something powerful that happens when we give voice to what we're feeling, but when those emotions have come up because of events that have taken place it isn't enough to just talk about it. Let's be honest, it can be very easy (and even cathartic) to lose your shit a bit and consider the anger managed - especially if you're someone who tends to bottle things up. But it's only half the remedy your heart is seeking.

Unmanaged Anger works in the same way but in reverse. It's all action, with a focus on feeling better, but without examining what's underneath. There are dozens of books that have been written on the subject and many will tell you to go scream in your car, punch a pillow, or take it out on the treadmill. Those are superficial fixes that have a place (they all move energy), but are not the end result on their own.

When anger builds it becomes like a pressure cooker where everything is bubbling and boiling within us and we know it needs to get out. And yeah, a scream session to Jagged Little Pill helps to alleviate that immediate pressure but it doesn't solve the underlying cause of what pissed you off in the first place.

Anger needs a strategy.

We know it's a cycle, and we can use the natural course that anger takes to learn about ourselves. We can see what our triggers are, what patterns we're repeating, what's most important to us, and where our boundaries lie. It's a powerful tool, if we allow it to be.

Identify it: In this phase, we're recognizing that things aren't alright, and we're opening up to the exploration of this emotion. This asks us to be willing, and to have courage, because sitting with anger is not an easy task.

Acknowledge it: In this phase we're being honest about what is coming up for us, what's underneath it, and any other emotions that are added into the mix. This asks us to be curious and push beyond the obvious or superficial so we can get to the heart of the matter.

Feel it: In this phase, it may get ugly. You're going to allow yourself, with zero judgment, to be with the emotions coming up: the anger and anything else that has hitched a ride. This asks us to have deep compassion for where we're at, and to accept ourselves in our less-than-Instagram-worthy moments.

Move it: In this phase, you're ready to let go. It's important not to skip the steps to get to this part, otherwise the learning doesn't happen. Once you've processed everything you can about what you're feeling, you can use tools to move the energy these emotions create within you. There is no one right way to move energy - use whatever works for you. Whether it's going for a run, meditating with crystals, scream-crying to 90s angst-rock, or something completely different: if it works, you're doing it right. You'll find a bunch of suggestions in Chapter 9.

Reflect on it: In this phase, you're ready to understand what's transpired. You've done the detective work of what you're feeling and allowed it to move through you, it's now time to assimilate that. In this phase, it's helpful to ask questions, again, with zero judgment, to understand what has happened before. Questions like: What did I learn about myself? Where has this happened before? What do I need to do to make sure it won't happen again? can give us a lot of insight into ourselves, and our tender hearts.

This is why it's important that we view anger as a sacred teacher, instead of something we sweep under the rug and avoid talking about in polite society. We need to normalize talking about the things that upset us so expressing anger (and every other uncomfortable emotion) is something so common place that we never feel the need to hold it back. And then, once we've called it out from the shadows and spoken it's name without shame, we need to come up with an action plan so we can decide what we're going to do with all of these feelings - to help them move through us, and to use them for good in the world, and for ourselves. It's anger alchemy.

Physical

Anger has a way of feeling like it's devouring us from the inside. It can have short and long term effects, depending on how habitual it is and how long it goes unmanaged. It's correlated with anxiety, high blood pressure, and tension pains (like headaches and sore backs and shoulders), which are often the gateway to more serious conditions.

Our nervous system takes cues from the body for how to respond, and being in a regular state of stress causes the brain to release more hormones to try to help manage what's going on. Our digestive system goes into overdrive, our sleep gets disrupted, we can feel depressed and it can even show up in our skin with conditions like eczema.

So imagine, we've decided to avoid dealing with an uncomfortable emotion which has a byproduct of all these other physical experiences which are also uncomfortable, making everything a bit harder to deal with. Not only that, but it has a compounding effect: nothing makes dealing with challenging situations harder like feeling pain, anxiety, and being under-rested. In short, we've got more stuff to be angry about, and less emotional capacity to cope with it because it's all a bit much.

Psychological

One of the hardest aspects of feeling angry for any given length of time, is the impact it can have on your mind. I mentioned anxiety before (which is not just physical, but also psychological), but there's also this feeling of losing the person you are.

When we become consumed by our anger it starts to distract us from the things that bring us joy, which is a core part of our mental health, and our sense of self. The psychological and physical go hand in hand: you want to feel right in your body, so you can feel right in your mind, so you can feel like yourself. (Because isn't getting lost in anger really just feeling like you aren't yourself at the end of the day?)

Talking with the right people can help. It's not just about finding a trained professional, but the right fit for you personally. Each professional's approach is different, so you need to find the one that makes you feel safe enough to dig into the stories and the emotions that are making you feel trapped in the anger loop.

Emotional

The stories we tell ourselves about our anger, and how we justify it, can really take our emotions for a ride. Not only do we have the heightened experience of anger, but we have residual feelings like shame, regret, depression, and so on that are tagging along for the right.

We need to experience life as who we are, not through the lens of how we're feeling. Remember: you feel your emotions, but they are not you. Emotions are just energy running through your body, taking up space in your head and your heart for a temporary time. We still need to be in the driver's seat.

Emotions also take up energy (some emotions more than others), and you have a finite amount to use every day. It's important that you're using your energy wisely, including learning from your anger so you can allow it to move through you, so that you're not stuck in a downward spiral for long.

Relationships

One of the hardest aspects of anger is how isolating it is for the person experiencing it.

There is such a breach of trust that happens – when it's your own anger, you may not trust yourself in situations you may find stressful (ie: most things in life), and when it's someone else's, it can be hard to trust yourself with them to not get set off.

The isolation can be the hardest part to recover from. This isn't work that can be done in a silo: we need mirrors to see this with, we need people to reflect back to us, and we need to be lovingly called out when we're being assholes. So when you find the people who can do that, hold on to them. Because this is deep, sacred work.

So right here, right now, I'm asking you to commit to these 3 things:

1. That when you feel something's up and it doesn't feel great, that you're willing to sit with it and see what it has to say.

2. That when you've learned from that feeling, that you'll allow it to be in your heart – even if it's uncomfortable, awkward, messy, or weird. You won't rush it's process and you'll trust yourself to move it when the time is right.

3. That after the anger has moved through you, you'll take some time for quiet contemplation to figure out why the hell it all happened in the first place, and what your takeaways were.

And if you wanna make it extra woo and ultra potent, write these commitments in your journal, on the night of a new moon, to powerfully declare to the Universe that you are ready to make anger your sacred teacher.

SACRED SOUL SEARCHING

Here are the reflection questions to take to your journal:

How does anger typically affect me? (Consider the impact on your physical, psychological, emotional, and relationship health)

After I've learned from it, what is the best way I can move anger through me, and why does it work?

Part 3
Growing Through Anger

CHAPTER 7

It's not about them, it's about you

Before we get into this section, I want to address a few things:

- Forgiveness is not some destination that you arrive at, or some goal you achieve.
- Forgiveness does not say that what they did (or what you did) is okay.
- Forgiving someone does not mean you have to have any kind of relationship with them.
- If your forgiveness doesn't include YOU, it's incomplete.

Forgiveness is a courageous, conscious choice. It's a willingness to look at a painful situation and choose to no longer let it hold power over you. It's a way of life that, if new to you, will take an adjustment period like any dietary change, exercise regime, or new habit you're trying to build. Now let's dig into each of those points a bit more.

Forgiveness is not some destination that you arrive at, or some goal you achieve.

Forgiveness is a lifestyle, an ongoing process and conscious choice that you can choose to make (or let's be honest: choose not to make). When we treat it as something we can check off a to-do list, or get a gold star, we set ourselves up for disappointment. It's not a "one and done" act, it's something we choose, and choose again.

A couple of years ago I attended an event in Las Vegas, and colour medium Dougall Fraser was one of the speakers. He talked about his relationship with forgiveness and how sometimes he had to forgive several times just over Christmas dinner.

When we look at it this way, it takes the pressure off of rushing the process. We allow it to happen on its own time, and we acknowledge that just because we're okay with it today, doesn't mean we will be tomorrow. All we can do is our best, and if we aren't holding ourselves to an impossible standard, it makes it easier on us not to slip and slide down a shame spiral when we don't get it right all the time.

Forgiveness does not say that what they did (or what you did) is okay.

A lot of our resistance to forgiveness is because we're worried that we're giving the person who hurt us carte blanche, which puts us at risk of being hurt again in the future. (And being mad or disappointed in ourselves because of it.) If I'm honest, a lot of people who have habitual behaviours that require forgiving will sometimes manipulate us into believing that we must forgive them, and in doing so, that it's resolved and doesn't have to be talked about ever again. (We'll talk more about them in the next section.)

And I get it – when we feel shameful about something we've done and we've hurt someone we love, we don't want to revisit that feeling over and over again. But it's not the person who has done the hurting that gets to choose when the feelings are resolved.

You need to set the pace. Your heart's healing is not something that can be rushed, even if the feelings that come with that heartache are wildly uncomfortable (for yourself, or the person you need to forgive).

When we forgive, what we are saying is that we're choosing to no longer let the actions of the past (by ourselves or someone else) impact how we choose to live our life today. That's it. It's not saying what they've done has gone away, and it hasn't minimized the harm that was done. It's taking back your power and living life on your own terms.

It needs to feel okay to you. If the word forgiveness still gives you the wiggins, let's just call it "letting go."

Forgiving someone does not mean you have to have any kind of relationship with them.

This is the one item on this list that will piss off the people who hurt you. Somewhere there's been this big misconception that if you forgive someone, it means you can go back to how things were. And that my sweet, is a big pile of horse dung.

If we reduce it to the most fundamental nugget, it's this: you get to choose who you do and do not have a relationship with. It's that simple. (Note: I didn't say it was that 'easy'.)

Sometimes, the people who hurt us think that

when we forgive them, it means they've wiped the slate clean. They've passed Go, they've collected their $200, so when we decide not to engage, it pisses them off. They thought forgiveness meant they were given a pass, and they're not ready to be held responsible for their actions. They will try to convince you that you have to have a relationship with them. They'll recruit other people to try to pressure you into having a relationship with them. Their #1 goal is to restore the status quo - which most likely also restores the power imbalance in the relationship, but I digress. Here's a big hint: most of the time, these are the people who are the most likely to reoffend. They haven't integrated the lesson, they're putting their ego, and their desire to not feel guilt, shame, or regret above your need for comfort or feelings of security. So fuck those guys, you owe them NOTHING.

That doesn't mean it won't be ultra uncomfortable when they pressure you, or use others to pressure you into re-engaging. Sometimes, you need to evaluate which discomfort is worse: the one where you go back to how things were with the person or people who hurt you (or allowed you to be hurt), or the one where you stand your ground, have to find a new community of people to surround yourself with, and may have to battle loneliness. This is especially hard when the re-offenders are family members - hard, but not impossible. But the point is this: it's YOUR choice to make. They don't get to choose for you, not anymore.

If your forgiveness doesn't include YOU, it's incomplete.

We hold so many stories about ourselves and have ultra-high expectations that aren't attainable, so when we screw up it's really easy to become hard on ourselves. I've even been a part of situations where both parties screwed up, and for some reason I find it easier to forgive them than it is to forgive myself. And that's tragic.

Having these Herculean expectations of ourselves puts so much pressure on us, in every aspect of life. We're expected to be the perfect children, the perfect employee, the perfect spouse - and perfection is just not achievable.

So when we can shelve those expectations, we create a lot of space for us to be regular old fallible humans. We have the capacity for deep compassion for ourselves, and any of the contributing factors that made us behave in a way that we feel we need to forgive.

Here's the thing: you're human, and you're going to fuck up every so often.

It's not messing up that's the problem, it's what we do after it. And creating a safe place for our humanity to be expressed, even on our own, without judgment or critique is a soothing balm for the soul. It's probably the greatest gift you can give yourself.

I know this section shifted the conversation a bit away from your anger and how to explore it, but because you're not the only person in your life who says and does things rooted in anger, it's really important to explore this facet as part of the discussion around anger. How other people's anger impacts you is entirely relevant, and you deserve to have this check in.

When it comes to forgiveness, I have some tools and strategies that have helped me work through a lot, whether it's in forgiving other people or forgiving myself. I encourage you to try these out, and certainly any others you find yourself drawn to, until you can find what works for you specifically.

Forgiveness by prayer

The first is a prayer from the Hawaiian tradition called ho'oponopono. Despite my best efforts I have yet to master the name of this prayer, however it's message is so simple and can create massive heart-shifts if you say it in earnest:

I'm sorry.
Please forgive me.
Thank you.
I love you.

You can think about the person or people you're forgiving and say this with so much love and compassion in your heart, imagining them surrounded in white light. I also like to imagine with this prayer that any energetic cords that are linking me to this person, place, or situation are dissolved with the words. And I'll be honest, it rarely works by saying it once. The most beautiful transformations I've witnessed with the ho'oponopono prayer are when I use it as a mantra. I will sit in a quiet meditation with my mala beads, really feeling into the situation with my heart, and then begin saying this prayer with each bead. After 108 times, the message can get through to the most stubborn of hearts.

Forgiveness as a declaration

Your words hold immense power - even if you don't consider yourself someone who is witchy or woo-y. There's a reason why we've heard so much about manifestations and even ritual or spell work over the years - all of this is your thoughts, feelings, words, and energy in action.

The beautiful thing is using declarations as a tool for forgiveness is accessible to everyone. It's not tied to dogma or organized religion - you can be 100% atheist and still use this strategy.

You'll want to choose words that are personal to you, as these can be the most effective. If you need some inspiration to start, here is a declaration you can use:

I am sovereign.
I am the chooser of my thoughts, feelings, and actions.
I choose only what is in my highest good. I leave no space for the rest.
I am whole, healed, and complete.

While it doesn't mention forgiveness specifically, choosing only what is in your highest good means you're choosing to be unencumbered by the events that required you to forgive. Whatever words you choose, say them with conviction, say them with a hand on your heart and your love beneath it. The more you believe it, the more likely it is to come true.

Now, you can also use the power of declaration if you know you'd like to forgive, but you're not quite there yet. I call this praying for the willingness.

When we are reluctant to let go of our hurt, even if we want to, it's easy to think the head has gotten the message and that it's the heart that's unwilling - but it's actually the opposite. Our heart is the purest part of ourselves, and the most tapped in aspect that's aligned with our highest good and truth. The heart is the part that says "I'd like to forgive" and it's usually the egoic parts of the head that says "...but I'm not ready."

In this case, I will spend every day for at least a month praying for the willingness. I will take a minute or two out of my day to declare that I'm feeling this hurt, but that I'm willing for that to change. And with enough time, and some focused intention, it has always eventually shifted. Often times faster than I'd expected.

Forgiveness with angelic support

My last support for any forgiveness work I do is calling on Archangel Jeremiel. Working with Jeremiel is how I saw how the ways I was able to release anger, hurt, and resentment towards other people but had carried it (plus a boat load of shame) for myself with zero hesitation or even consideration to do otherwise. I have to be honest: while I have a few deeply rooted anger seeds that are tougher to dig up and release, as a general rule I find it pretty easy to forgive other people, but struggle to hold myself to the same standards. By working with Jeremiel, this is slowly shifting.

Working with the angels isn't some distant faraway thing that's reserved for the chosen few. Angels are non-denominational beings of love, who walk alongside us every day. They're happy to support our journey if we open our hearts and ask.

You can invite Jeremiel into your meditation by imagining a beam of golden, honey-coloured light coming from your heart's centre. Before you, in front of the beam of light appears Jeremiel, who you can ask to realign or recalibrate you so you are able to restore your heart to its natural state of forgiveness, openness, and readiness to receive. You can hand over any of the hurt, resentment or anger you're feeling, and ask him to lift it from every cell of your being. If meditation isn't your jam, you can also say a prayer to Jeremiel, either as part of your regular practice, or as you're working through a particular event that requires forgiving. Your prayer can be as simple as:

Thank you Jeremiel for reminding me
how to forgive, and for realigning the vibration
of my heart to its natural state of love.
I hand over the hurt, the anger, the sadness,
and the resentment that I carry.
I am lighter. I am freer. I am safe.
Thank you, thank you, thank you.

Forgiveness by ritual

While there's been a shift in our culture to be less about the connection that ritual and ceremony bring and more about the avoidance and distraction of a Netflix queue and social media feed, there's still a part of us on a cellular level that recognizes the significance of intentionally marking an occasion. We've somehow only made time for ritual for marking major lifestones like weddings and funerals, but this same sacred container can be applied to anything.

While I have many ritual tools at my disposal, when I have an emotion to transmute (and often that emotion is anger), fire is my ritual tool of choice. When I first started doing fire ceremonies I didn't even recognize what I was doing was a ritual. It started after a particularly bad break up, where I was a mixed-bag of emotions. I felt everything from betrayal, to disappointment, heartbreak, anger, sadness, longing and loneliness, the list went on and on. I decided to make a list of everything I wanted to release myself from with regards to the relationship. I chose to keep all the good stuff, so I could still keep my heart open and hopeful for my future love, but I didn't want to hold onto the hurt that came with that relationship's ending.

It felt essential that I used plain white paper here to maintain the purity of my intentions and the integrity of the work (it's still something I hold on to, but do whatever works for you). I'd cut the paper up into many pieces, and on one side I wrote his name, and on the other, the emotion I wanted to release myself from in relation to our relationship. I then put a candle in a metal bowl, kept some water close by, and proceeded to do a little fire ceremony outside, under a tree in the moonlight. One by one, I would take the papers in hand and make the declaration, "By burning this paper, I release myself from the [emotion] I feel towards [ex boyfriend's name]" And then I'd place the paper in the fire, watch it burn, take a moment to allow the energy to move, and then carry onto the next one.

All of this was done with love and gratitude in my heart, as a way to bring some closure to us both. It's important to note that this wasn't something I did immediately post-break up. But after a couple of weeks of reflection and the sadness still lingering, I decided I'd extracted all that I could from the experience, and it was time to move on. It's not a process you want to rush into because there are lessons in our darker times, but there's a big difference from still processing your pain and just wallowing in it. (I say this as a former wallower.)

However you choose to shift the energy, stepping into the vibration of forgiveness will restore your heart to its natural state bringing you peace of mind, and more ease, clarity and freedom. And if you can't get there on your own that's absolutely okay too.

Inner work vs Outside help

There are some myths I've seen run rampant in spiritual circles that I'd like to address:

1. You shouldn't cut toxic family members out of your life. You should look at why they trigger you, learn from them, and be grateful for the role they have in your life.
2. You should be able to solve everything imaginable with yoga, herbs, essential oils, meditation, etc. If you've tried everything and it hasn't worked, you just haven't found the right thing yet.
3. Inner work is a solitary journey. Sometimes you need to run away to Bali, or do regular Vipassanas, or just journal a whole lot more, but the answers you seek are within you and only YOU have the key to unlock them.

Let's talk about why that's a whole lot of bullshit.

Myth 1 BUSTED: You don't need to talk to toxic people. When I started writing this book, I wasn't on speaking terms with many of my family members, and I've taken a lot of heat for it. I've been called ungrateful, told that I have my head in my ass, and was described as someone who is "not a good person".

I am Teflon - because bullshit stories like those are what keep people stuck with their abusers every day. In my case, I'd rather face criticisms that I know in my heart of hearts are not true, than have to deal with the ongoing manipulation, judgment, competition, and favouritism that was involved with maintaining these relationships.

If when you spend time with a person you feel worse for it, those are not your people, even if you're biologically related. It's not a decision you have to make lightly - after all, you want to be able to look yourself in the mirror and say "Yeah, I made the right choice for me." at the end of the day. But if you're digging in and doing your own work and the people around you aren't, sometimes you need to minimize contact or remove them altogether. Fearless boundaries are the biggest self love declaration I know of.

Myth 2 BUSTED: While I'm a firm believer in taking a natural approach to everything, sometimes, you need a great doctor with a prescription pad. This is especially frowned upon in the spiritual community - even our naturopathic community in Canada is divided between NDs who write prescriptions and NDs who do not.

But let's be real - if you have a chemical imbalance in your brain, which can be caused by a number of things but most likely your genetics, no amount of lavender oil is going to make you happy. (And I say that as someone trained in aromatherapy.) Lifestyle changes, dietary changes, and physical exercise can do WONDERS to support your body as it's processing emotions like anger, but when you've tried them and they didn't work, sometimes you need to broaden your horizons a little.

Having a neurochemical imbalance is no different to being a diabetic who struggles with keeping regular insulin levels - we don't think they've done anything wrong, and we don't expect them to regulate it entirely with chanting and crystals. We make sure they get the drugs they need so they can navigate life with as much balance as possible. There is zero shame in needing medication, whether it's for the short or long term. Self care is making the choices that support your highest and greatest good, and if it takes medication to do that, then it should at least be something you consider. (And if anyone tries to shame you for taking meds, they go into that category of people in Myth 1. Fuck those guys.)

Myth 3 BUSTED: Ultimately, inner work is solitary work - you need to take responsibility for exploring your shadows, your stories, and your truths to decide what does and doesn't work for you any more. However it's pretty unlikely you're taking the journey alone. Every book you read, every event you attend, every online program you sign up for contributes to your inner work journey. It's the coaches you work with, the energy healers, the body workers, even your therapist. Yes, the reflection you do may be solitary, but you are no lone wolf. And anyone who tells you that you have to be is either full of it or trying to sell you something.

We are social creatures and we thrive on feedback, so if we don't have someone to riff off of it really limits our abilities to explore and process our inner worlds. When you do inner work in a bubble, you're really limited to how far you can take your journey - it really helps to have someone who has been there before, or has a different view point. If you consider an explorer who is adventuring through new terrain, they can bushwhack their way through the jungle, guided only by their compass and whatever they can see in front of them. Or they can do it with a map in hand, written by someone who has been there and done that. Or they can take the journey with the help of an experienced guide who knows what to expect and what to look out for. Sure, doing it alone the explorer gets the bragging rights of making it on their own. But they may miss out on the best views, the best food, or they may stumble into dangerous terrain and not get to tell the tale at all.

There is zero shame in getting the help you need to work through whatever it is you're feeling. The only way to do it wrong is to suffer silently by yourself because you're afraid to ask.

Each of these myths is a form of spiritual bypassing, which is effectively trying to "love and light" away anything that isn't a perfect happy disposition. Even when you're living the high vibe life, shitty things happen, and to deny them or to dismiss them as untrue because they aren't instagram worthy and may make people uncomfortable is to weaponize spirituality.

There are not enough conversations happening about spiritual bypassing right now, so if you see it in action please do call it out. It's a terribly deceptive type of manipulation, even when it's done with supposed good intentions, because it sounds so true and so believable that it can be easy to buy into. (Especially when the emotion they're dismissing is one you don't want to experience anyways.)

Honour your feelings, give yourself the time to process, and do whatever feels right for you. You get to set the terms of how you navigate your anger and any other emotion you may be experiencing.

Including men in the conversation

In the last decade or two there has been a beautiful rise in the personal development world that has helped women and gender non-conforming folks to claim their power and start building the lives of their dreams. We started seeking purpose beyond our families and our work, and we started looking within and beginning to explore what was underneath. We read the books (thank you Oprah), went to the events and the rallies, and started to speak up and show up like never before. As a woman, I've got my pom poms out and cheering like a crazy person... but as an observer of the human condition, I'm also a bit cautious in how excited I'll allow myself to get.

Because a rising means there's disruption.

Now before you pull out your pitchforks or pussy hats, please know that I'm not opposed to disruption. The same-old, same-old isn't working for the large majority of our population, and things need to change. Not just so the distribution of power shifts, but so that people feel safe, feel valued, feel seen and heard. My concern is for the pendulum to swing too far in the other direction, where we still have systems of power and inequality, but with different people on top.

Let me explain with a story from my days working in a neurofeedback clinic.

I spent 3 years balancing and harmonizing brainwaves, which would support people with various brain-based challenges like depression, anxiety, insomnia, an inability to focus, and so on. Oftentimes when a client who was in a romantic partnership would come in, shortly after our time together we'd witness either big changes in their relationships. Either they'd start therapy together, or the relationship would end, or they'd come up with some new ground rules for what was and wasn't acceptable anymore. Their change was disruptive, the way things used to be were no longer working, so they had to shift or the relationship needed to end. The disruption was both a powerful declaration of self love and a great act of self preservation.

In some cases the partner would come in for sessions and then after their program the couple could work together to create a new reality together. What a beautiful position to be in, right? However oftentimes there would be too much hurt and resentment, and the partner would rather walk away than do the work themselves. And that's sadly just how free will works. We can't want change for someone else enough to make it happen.

Which brings me back to this disruption in our society right now. Because the large majority of the people on the self-help train are women, they're having these epiphanies and shifting and growing which is shaking things up in their homes, their offices, and their communities. Now, the average white man who is used to being "Top Dog" has been gradually stripped of his power, and he hasn't had much say in it, or much support through the process. This is the way it's been for so long, not just for him, for the generations before him, so not only is he angry that it's happening, but he's also a bit lost about what to do next.

So what does he do? He acts out, he tries to find ways to restore the balance of power, and it's often done with anger, intimidation, and pressure. All of the things that caused this uprising in the first place.

Not only has he not been given the same access to inner work that women have, it's never even occurred to him to do it because there has never been a need. We aren't raising boys to talk about their feelings, and we're allowing them to grow up into these expressions of toxic masculinity who are struggling to keep their grip on whatever power they can find, however they can find it.

But these tactics: anger, fear-mongering, intimidation, and pressure aren't working anymore. Women are rising fearlessly like never before, and with the dissolution of the traditional family dynamic (the man working and the woman staying home with the kids), women are needing men less and less. And the men are feeling it.

Since the 1950s, men are 3 to 5 times more likely to die by suicide than women. While there hasn't been a lot of clarity on the exact cause of the gender disaparity with suicide, one of the theories is that the traditional gender dynamics put a lot of stress on men as providers, and they haven't been taught healthy ways to manage it. If we look at modern times, on top of the stress, there's a despair that comes with feeling powerless.

Now – the purpose of this section isn't to feel sorry for the older white man archetype. The biggest challenge in even writing this chapter is that with these people being the biggest perpetrators of trauma for women, people of colour, and marginalized people of all genders, is being able to park my personal feelings and bias and look at what's happening objectively.

We are in a beautiful epoch where we can make change, offer support, show new ways things can be done. We've been doing that these last couple of years by fostering sisterhood and helping each other out... perhaps it's time to include men in this work. In most cases I expect these sacred spaces need to be spearheaded by conscious men who have dug into this already on their own, but we need to work through our own wounds, and our own anger, so that co-ed spaces feel safe and sacred for people of all genders.

Let's be realistic - some of these men are too stubborn, and too determined to hold onto the old ways of being, and they'll keep a tight grip on the past. These are not the ones we can help. But for the ones that are willing? They need the same support, the same access to resources, and the same hand up that we were given at the start of our journeys. This isn't to create a more conscious version of the old way, but creating a new reality where we can work together in a balance of both the divine feminine and masculine. Because we truly are better together.

SACRED SOUL SEARCHING

Here are the reflection questions to take
to your journal:

*How do I know when I'm ready to forgive?
(Does this change when the forgiveness
is for myself? If so, how?)*

*How can I choose to forgive, so I'm no
longer held back by past events?*

CHAPTER 8
What makes anger sacred?

When I first started writing this book, it didn't have a title. I kept referring to it as *The Anger Book*, and sometimes I would add the little orange faced emoji to emphasize the point. Whenever someone would ask me what it was about (because anger's a massive topic on it's own), I'd say "It's an exploration of anger as a sacred teacher." So now that we've dug into many of anger's facets, we're ready to explore and learn from the divinity within it.

Ego Vs. Essence

At the start of my journey I worked with a spiritual teacher for 5 years, and one of the first lessons he taught was that there are two paths in life: ego, and essence. You can distill all of life into this dichotomy. It doesn't take a rocket scientist to know which camp anger falls into.

If we simplify this a little, I like to imagine a fork in the road, and to the left of it is a sign that says 'Love' and to the right the sign reads 'Everything Else'. It really is that simple. So when we remove all the judgments we have about our anger- we drop the shame, the blame, the hurt, the injustice, all of it - what's left is a separation from love.

Love is your purpose. Honestly, experiencing love is all we've come here to do. Giving, receiving, witnessing love.

When we give into the primal expressions of anger (I'm talking the all-consuming rage that we're not in the space to learn from or reflect on), we are not in our hearts - even when the thing we're angry about has to do with someone or something we love and hold dear. Now on top of whatever it is that made us mad in the first place, we're also experiencing the loss and distance from the very thing we came here to experience in this lifetime.

So what do we do?

The first step is having the awareness that we've gone down the other fork in the road, and that we've strayed from love. We need to acknowledge this, but with great love and compassion for ourselves. (This is a "no judgement, no drama" zone. None of this is good or bad - it is, what it is.)

The second step is choosing to head back. Take a few deep breaths to bring you back into the present moment. When you feel ready, say the words "I choose love now." As you do, tap each finger to your thumb on each word, making a short series of mudras. (I - pointer, choose - middle, love - ring, now - pinky) This is the type of activity that's very discreet - you can do it under the desk when your bossy coworker is saying something that pisses you off - and can help you to actively choose something other than anger, even when the opportunity to go off the path to love presents itself.

Anger as a teacher

If you're anything like I used to be, when you're in the aftermath of having been really angry you feel kind of hungover. Energy is ultra low, regret is high, and you may still be piecing together what was said and done in the heat of the moment.

No judging here, beauty, I've been there.

I'd usually try to have a nap to sleep off the discomfort, then wake up and try to get on with the rest of my day. Which from a release perspective got stuff done – all of that energy that boiled inside me had an outlet. But from an inner work and learning perspective, the lesson was entirely lost on me.

Anger is a sacred teacher.

It shows you what is left to heal – even when you've done so much work on those things that you think there can't possibly be more to do. It shines a light on the unexplored parts of ourselves that were too uncomfortable to look at, so we pushed them down, buried them, and denied them. Lightworkers are SO GOOD at denying the darkness. We dismiss it as 'low vibe' and we believe that if we look at it and accept it as something that's happening, that we'll attract more of it. But if we aren't digging into that stuff, there's no work going on at all. We become *Lightplayers* – we know all the right things to say, but there's nothing actually being DONE about it. It's all lip service with no call to action.

In the early days of my marriage, my husband and I would be sitting on the couch, side by side, on our laptops. He's a digital artist, so he spends a lot of his evenings working on code for a project, or researching new ways to do things. I spent a lot of my time working on content to batch for social media, catching up with friends in various time zones, and streaming Netflix. Whenever I'd start talking to him, he'd often be so in the zone that he didn't hear me, or he'd only heard half of what I was saying, and it would make me so angry. On the surface, I felt like I was competing for his attention with his devices, and that his art was more important than our marriage. Anger isn't a rational emotion, so it has a knack for temporarily erasing all evidence I have to the contrary, and also ignores the fact that just seconds before, I was completely consumed with my own device – but I digress.

Over the first couple years of our marriage, I realized that this one thing kept coming up, and I kept being angry. Even though when I wasn't "in it" I could see all the ways he cherished our marriage, and me, and how loved and supported I was. (And the hypocrisy of ignoring him when I'm in the middle of something too.) So I decided to dig in. Because when something keeps coming up, and it doesn't get any less intense, you know there's a lesson at play here.

As a kid, I was teased and often dismissed for talking too much. My parents called me Gabby Guts and Motor Mouth and it absolutely destroyed me. To me, I was just an expressive kid, but to them, I was a bit (a lot) much. The irony is, the more I was ignored and dismissed, the more attention I craved, so the more I'd talk. It was a vicious, self perpetuating cycle that created a lot of separation for me, and feelings of rejection. This is a wound that followed me into my high school years, and even into my work in my early 20s. So when my husband would tune out, naturally it was like someone tore off the bandage and exposed the wound – and it hurt.

Seeing this shifted so much for me! Suddenly I wasn't looking for him to be my only sounding board, I started finding other outlets – friends, my blog, posting on social media, even this book. I also learned to ask "Are you in the zone?" before just jumping in and expecting him to drop everything to sometimes talk about nothing. And when I forget (because I'm human, so I sometimes forget), I listen to his unconscious cues (he gives a little sigh when I break his flow and he doesn't even realize it) and catch myself, without taking it personally.

And then... I started getting better about my own boundaries. Part of my resentment was that when he'd interrupt what I was doing, I'd drop everything to listen, and then lose my own flow. Suddenly, I started honouring myself better, and he'd ask if I was in the zone. When I'm in my office with the door closed, he never barges in - he always taps lightly to make sure he's not interrupting something. But none of this would have been possible if I wasn't willing to look at the feelings underneath my anger, then dig deeper to see why they were there in the first place. My willingness to face short term discomfort has paid off for years and years in my marriage.

Anger as a mirror

I went to an event a couple of years ago that featured a beautiful exercise where we were asked to think about a woman we really admired, and to think about the things about her we thought were so great. We were then asked to do the same with a woman who really triggered us, and ask ourselves about all the reasons why she gets under our skin. The woman leading the exercise then wrapped up by telling us that we have both of those elements within us: all the things we appreciated and admired, and all the stuff that kind of pissed us off.

Anger can be used in the exact same way.

There is a root in what we hate that resonates for us for some reason, and when we can identify what that is we can work on it – but not a second before. Women have a lot of internalized misogyny that we've inherited. So it's very easy to get catty, gossip, blame other women, or make assumptions about them – because it's a lot easier than accepting there's a part of us that hates women, even though we are women.

Despite being raised by parents who considered themselves feminists, on the subject of rape, the first stories I heard were that a lot of women 'cry rape' to get out of sticky situations, or to cover up regret for a decision they made. We know now that 1 out of 4 women have been sexually assaulted in their lifetime – that's 25% of us. But the idea that more often than not, allegations are false is what boys learned (through social conditioning, and from being around other boys and men – not the most valid sources of information on this subject), and girls were taught.

To this day, when I hear of stories of assault, I still have the knee jerk reaction to understand the situation first, especially when the accused is someone whose work I previously liked and admired. From there, I check myself. I remind myself that this is internalized misogyny and remember that, statistically, it's less damaging for me to believe a survivor and occasionally get it wrong, than I am to believe a perpetrator and occasionally get it right.

This same internalized misogyny is how we treat other women like our competition, instead of like our sisters. Because so long as we're fighting each other, we're not fighting the patriarchal systems that remain in place. In-fighting keeps a lot of people in the same place, and the power systems in their current state.

But unless we've received a PhD in gender studies, we haven't been taught to explore any of this. We don't even see this internalized hatred and rejection of our own selves, which we need to do in order to be able to do this work. When we look at the things that piss us off as mirrors for something inside that needs a deeper examination, we can heal so much.

Now, a lot of people in my circles will take this into spiritual realms and look for correlating ties in previous lives we've experienced with things like past life regression or the Akashic Records. I completely understand the healing that can come from this, they're part of my coaching work as well, but I'd really like to challenge you to stick in this incarnation to fully reap the benefits of this exercise.

When you're feeling angry, especially at another person (but also at yourself), here are some things you can ask yourself:

What is it I'm angry about right now?
Where do I see myself in this?
How does this play out in my life?
What work do I need to do?
What support do I need?

Anger as a symptom of a need for change

When I was in college, I had a customer service job in a call center, and the job required zero actual customer service. The goal was to prevent giving refunds, so the parameters we could actually help within were very small and very strict. We were permitted to be rude, and had very little supervision.

Suddenly, I had an outlet for everything I suppressed in the years of "being good". My goal (and I say this with very little pride here) was to always push the envelope as far as I could, to make people angry, but to not actually swear at them or call them names. To be honest, at that time, it was kinda fun. I was so exhausted from being an overachiever, and a lifetime people pleaser, that being paid to be a snarky bitch felt like the biggest gift ever.

As the school year was getting closer to ending, and I'd be starting a career in broadcasting in another city, I started to get itchy. Suddenly instead of delighting in rude customers I could torment, they started making me mad. And two days before what was to be my last day because I was moving away, I broke my one cardinal rule. When an angry customer said "Fuck you", I yelled back and said "Well fuck you too, sir." (Yes, I even added the 'sir' at the end.) I immediately resigned, because I knew my time there was done.

Anger becomes a symptom that something needs to change.

Anyone who has stayed at a job for too long can relate to this. Suddenly the mundane crap you'd put up with day in and day out is suddenly so frustrating, and so infuriating.

Anyone who has stayed in a relationship for too long can relate to this. Suddenly all the little annoying habits your partner has go from kinda quirky, to rage inducing.

Here's the thing though: you haven't made the change yet, no matter what signs you're seeing. You're afraid you're not ready, that it'll be too much, too hard. I get it. But here's the beautiful thing... your discomfort says you're ready. If you weren't, it wouldn't matter so much. So the only thing missing is YOU realizing that you're ready.

And on that point: ready for change doesn't necessarily mean burning it all to the ground. (Cue the ending of Office Space where Milton burns Initech down.) Change can mean ending, but a lot of the time it means a transition. With work, maybe you need a new position, or to ask for extra support on your team. In relationships, maybe you try doing things differently, see a counselor, or get some time away together.

Don't fear the change, it's something pretty

exciting on the horizon. And if not for feeling pissed off, you may not even know just how badly you need it. So really you should be saying: "Thanks, anger."

Anger as a sign your boundaries have been crossed

Attention all people pleasers: it is your job to create and uphold your boundaries.   I know you want to be nice, you don't want to inconvenience anyone, and you want to be liked... but you can't do all of that at a cost to your own well being.

We are all responsible for our own boundaries and their enforcement. We can't expect other people to read our minds, or assume that they just know where our boundaries are. Especially when those boundaries will shift and change and grow as we do. It's an evolution of who we are, so we need to be in regular communication with the people around us to make sure that everyone knows what the rules of engagement are. We are the gatekeepers of our energy.

Recently I had one of my coaching clients reach out asking technical questions about how to implement things on the website her designer was building. At the time, we weren't actively working together, but in the past, I wasn't firm about my boundaries and would help people beyond their packages regularly. (Via text on my personal phone number, during off-hours, out of scope work, and in between packages.) Through my own inner work, I had started to clarify and firm up my own boundaries about how I use and value my time. So when I replied to her, I had to let her know that she'd need to direct these types of questions to her web designer as we were not currently working together. Not going to lie: it was hard. This is a client I adore and consider a friend, but it was necessary work for both of us. And now our relationship is so much stronger for it, and when she has technical questions she brings them to her coaching calls.

How did I know the boundary had been crossed? My initial reaction to reading her text was "Ugh, why is she sending this to me - we're not even working together right now?!" which cued a moment to reflect before replying. She had no way of knowing I'd been doing all this inner work behind the scenes, particularly around boundaries, and that I was firming up my energy exchanges in my work. Because I'd had that realization that she wasn't doing anything especially wrong, she was following the lead I'd originally set with my lack of boundaries, I was able to reply with so much love but also with a firm honouring of what was acceptable now.

I get it - when someone oversteps it can feel maddening, especially when we haven't yet seen how we've contributed to it happening. (And let's be honest, some people are just boundary-pushers, so we may need to be more discerning about who we engage with.) There are so many contributing factors: age, culture, gender and so on that contribute to how we engage with people and what we expect to be okay when it hasn't been stated otherwise. We have a knack for expecting that people's boundaries are the same as ours, so when they behave differently, we unconsciously make up a story about them, or about ourselves, about why this has happened. That's where the feelings of anger, frustration, and resentment come in. (And if I'm honest, a little self pity.)

The truth is that the majority of these situations could be resolved with some healthy communication - but we haven't been taught how to understand and express our boundaries in any kind of healthy way, and so we often wait until they've been crossed. And when we're recovering people-pleasers, we're so used to dismissing our boundaries in favour of perceived love, acceptance, and inclusion. So this becomes really big work to do. It's a powerful reclamation of our power and a declaration that we are so worth it.

Here are some questions you can ask yourself if you feel your boundaries have been crossed:

What boundary has been crossed here?
Did I know this boundary existed?
How did it feel when it was crossed?
What's underneath that feeling?
Have I expressed that boundary
implicitly to others? Why/why not?
How can I express this boundary
implicitly to others?

Anger is a journey, not a destination.

Here's the truth: anger isn't something you just figure out one day, it's a lifelong journey you take with yourself. Even someone doing their PhD exploring anger will tell you that. It's not something you can fully unpack with textbooks, it's a visceral, emotional, ongoing process that needs to be experienced to be fully understood.

Understanding how you truly feel, including uncomfortable emotions like anger, is to know yourself with more depth and intimacy. And the better your relationship is with yourself, the better your relationships with other people become. You begin asking for what you need. You express your boundaries and uphold them, and deal with things as they come up, long before they become big, explosive outbursts that everyone involved has to eventually heal from.

It's time to get comfortable with being in anger so that you can learn and grow from it. There is so much we lose by avoiding this sacred work, but when we can shift our perception of it and truly accept it as a sacred teacher it becomes a lot easier to wade into, and we become a lot less afraid of its depth. Now - instead of being intimidated or overwhelmed by it - we get curious, we become willing to explore, and we become students. Which is essential to our growth. Those states of intimidation are when we shut down, avoid, and distract ourselves. It's why we deem anger to be something so uncomfortable and inconvenient. By shifting that story to anger being a lesson instead, we become open and receptive. Which is where the learning begins.

Anger isn't a destination you're going to arrive at - it's something that needs continual exploration and a commitment to the discomfort it brings, particularly in the early days. But each time it flares up, it is a beautiful invitation to return to love... and it's there for you, whenever you choose to accept it.

SACRED SOUL SEARCHING

Here are the reflection questions to take to your journal:

Thinking back to the last time you were angry, what in that situation was being reflected back to you? What did you learn about yourself?

When was the last time your anger was calling on you to change something? How did you respond to it? How did that feel to experience?

CHAPTER 9
Dealing with anger

Most of the books that have been written about anger are all about this topic - how do you deal with anger. And because whole books have been focused on just this one topic, this will be the longest chapter in the book and also the one you're most likely to need to reference.

As you saw back in Chapter 6, there's a cycle to follow so that you are not just moving the anger but growing through it.

Because the process of feeling and reflecting on anger can be so uncomfortable, especially when we haven't learned how to cope with it, we tend to skip ahead to dealing with it. The beauty of dealing is that it's active, it gives our mind something to focus on instead of the discomfort of how we're feeling about the situation. So while it's definitely a necessary part of the process, I really encourage you to follow the cycle in order so that you're getting the most out of your experience. By now in this book you can see the rich lessons that are available through this process, and why it's essential to do them in order.

With all of that said, let's talk about dealing with anger.

Dealing with your anger

In Chapter 6 we went in depth about each phase of the cycle and how to use each phase to process your anger. And that's the heady, intellectualized part of the process. But right now I want to speak to your heart.

When we take the time to get real about what we're feeling, why we're feeling it, and where this has come up for us before, we're not just processing the anger as an emotion - we're getting to know ourselves better. We need to then find an outlet that will allow us to process the anger as an energy. There are some suggestions later in this chapter, but it can honestly be as simple as stopping what you're doing to take the time to breathe. Long, deep, relaxing breaths boost our brain's alpha waves and give our nervous system the cue that it doesn't need to be on alert. That simple step can then help us do something with our anger instead of being all consumed by it.

By the time we move into the reflective part of the Sacred Anger Strategy, we get to not only extract the lessons, but forgive ourselves for what we said and did in that moment. It's all about accepting the consequences of our actions, making right what is possible to make right and always doing your best. (But please remember, your 'best' is always changing, so you may handle things differently from one situation to the next. And that's okay - it's just part of being human.)

Dealing with other people's anger

The advice I'm about to give is for the everyday average situation, not when someone's safety is at risk. If you or someone else is in danger, please make sure you get the right support you need to be safe, which is something that a book just can't deliver.

When it is possible, the greatest gift you can give to someone who is in a state of anger is a space of non judgment. If their anger is directed at you and you're able to not take it personally, this becomes something you can unpack together afterwards, and has the potential to bring you closer. Though it's not an easy feat in many cases. (See above, re: being human.)

It's very possible, unless they've done a ton of inner work, that in the moment they're not ready to work through the strategies that are in this book. So your job in this situation isn't to help them resolve and learn from their anger, but to hold space as they manage it in the way they know how.

If you can give them empathy, and validation where it's appropriate, they will feel seen and heard, which can do so much for the heart. Especially if the anger is a mask for something that feels more vulnerable, or when their inner child is in the driver's seat. That being said, it's still important that you're upholding your boundaries, and that you know within yourself what is and isn't acceptable before it happens. This is the space of do no harm, but take no shit. No one should ever ask you to martyr yourself, and you must always honour what feels right and what feels comfortable above all else.

The importance of a judgment-free space is so key here. Anger brings out some pretty raw and unfiltered emotions. We can question if we're being unreasonable (even when we aren't), we can feel shame, and we can get so angry at ourselves for being in that space in the first place. They are judging themselves plenty, so by being able to love them in this state and not contribute to their shame spirals, you are gifting them something they're not able to give to themselves.

When it gets a bit much

Last summer I spent some time by the ocean in California. It was a gorgeous, hot sunny day on the beach, and we'd chosen a spot along the beach that was marked with "No Swimming" signs because the rip tide was so strong it had the capacity to pull you away. The surfers were there, and they gave the whole setting a dreamy feel, so we decided to stick around, even though we couldn't actually swim there.

We could go into the water though, and I chose to just be there, in the waves, wet feet in the sand to just be with the forces of nature, expressed through each crash of the waves. I found myself turning it into a bit of a game, digging my feet in, resisting the waves, almost defiantly daring them to try to knock me over.

What was interesting was that the waves that would shake my footing were never the ones that I expected. When a big, white frothy wave would come, I'd find myself bracing in preparation, and then nothing major would really happen. It was the covert waves that would get me... usually the smaller ones, less showy waves that would sneak in after the big ones. I don't know if it's because they came in after the big ones and I'd used a lot of my energy there, or if it's because they were more unexpected and I underestimated them, but they were typically the ones that would knock me over a bit.

The smaller waves also tended to travel in packs, so instead of it being one big strong wave it would be a series of smaller waves that would be harder to keep up with, and suddenly it became a challenge to stay upright.

And isn't it the same with life's challenges? You have one major thing happen, and it's hard but you can stay steady and keep to the course. But when you have small challenge after small challenge hitting you back to back in this series of microassaults, it can become a lot harder to not completely lose your shit. It can be hard to keep a steady footing when life keeps trying to knock you off your feet.

Trust me when I say I get it.

So let's explore some different supports that you can use to help you deal with anger (and all of the other emotions that linger behind it.) I'm giving you some of the tools that I like to work with, yours may look different, and if they're working, they're exactly right for you. I've chosen to share the things that are not necessarily best practices, but stuff I can personally vouch for to give you a good starting point if you aren't sure where to begin.

Nourish your vessel

How our body feels plays a vital role in how we're able to manage everything life throws at us, including anger. Drinking enough water is huge because we're made of water, and it holds vibrations, so staying hydrated gives us the physical ability to move that energy through us.

Sleeping well is also key, and sometimes when I'm really in it I will put myself to bed so I can wake up with a bit more calm and a steadiness to dig into whatever the anger created. If I'm exhausted, it's so much harder to get to the learning. Everything feels harder really, so having good sleep overall or taking a nap when emotions run high can be the break you need to keep on going.

The foods we eat can help us to ground our energy as well, in particular foods like red meat, root vegetables and dark chocolate. I'll speak more about grounding later in this chapter, but for now what you need to know is that if you've made it through the highest parts of anger, being able to do the inner processing can be a lot easier if you're grounded into your body.

Move your vessel

Moving your body is such an essential part of self-care, and it keeps us tapped into our physical form in ways that we can't really achieve by staying still. If meditation is about connecting with our higher realms, movement is what brings us back to earth.

How you move is entirely up to you – the only criteria is that it should feel good, and be safe. You can go for a run, punch a speed bag, dance ecstatically, take a long hike or do yoga. What you do doesn't matter as much as how it feels, and if it brings you some relief.

Some people feel they need to do it aggressively, maybe listening to angry music. While others use their movements to bring their energy back down, the solo time in the quiet to process what has happened, and the breath that comes from being active to recalibrate their nervous system.

I trust you, as an intuitive being (whether you realize that or not) to know what works for you. And if you find yourself curious about a particular movement, I encourage you to try it out before you're looking for an outlet for anger, because it may be just what you need when times get hard.

Music

The interesting thing about music is that there's no recipe for what will help you move your anger. While some people need loud, high energy music to help them feel like they're moving it, others need the exact opposite. Something soothing that will guide them back to their heart is the medicine they most need.

For me, I tend to gravitate to music that is associated with the hardest and angriest parts of my life. Remember earlier when I mentioned my inner Ruth Langmore – these would be her favourite songs, so she gets to feel unleashed. If you head to sacredangerbook.com you'll be able to hear and follow the Spotify playlist that I created for writing this book.

Angels

A lot of my coaching works with sacred messengers, and the angels are one of the biggest supports in my personal and professional practices. While there isn't an angel for anger specifically, because it's not the vibration they operate in, there are angels we can call on to work with the emotions that contribute to our anger and sometimes the aftermath that ensues.

This section is your guide to these messengers, but don't put pressure on yourself to memorize all of them. Angels aren't attached to recognition, so if you need help with one of the stages of your Sacred Anger Strategy and you can't think of who to call on, a blanket invitation to all angels to help will make sure you get the support you need.

Now let's look at some of the biggest supports we can call on individually for angelic guidance:

Archangel Gabriel - if you're feeling you aren't being heard, or are struggling to honour your truth, Gabriel can help you tap into your voice so you can speak up and be heard. Gabriel can also help you if you find yourself in the space of struggling to find the words for a heartfelt apology if anger has gotten the best of you.

Archangel Jeremiel - if you have work to do around forgiveness (someone who you've wronged, someone who has wronged you, or self-forgiveness), Jeremiel can help wash the waves of forgiveness over you. If you find yourself unwilling to forgive, you can also ask Jeremiel to help you open your heart to the willingness to forgive, so that it's something you can work towards, when it's not readily available for you right now.

Archangel Michael - if you've had your sense of safety shaken - by your actions, or the actions of others - Michael is the angel who can support you in feeling secure again. A lot of times we think of our safety and sense of security as being things related to physical attacks or transgressions, but this can be anything that contributed to not feeling steady, safe, and secure in the world.

Archangel Raguel - if a relationship is involved in the anger aftermath, Raguel is the angel who can support you in mending the relationship - whether it's a friendship, romantic partnership, or even a colleague. Speaking from experience, I find Raguel especially supportive for parents who are trying to navigate their relationship with their children, especially in the teen years.

Archangel Haniel - if you've found yourself having a hard time honouring your feelings, or your boundaries, Haniel is the angel who can help you get to the core of your heart's truth. This is particularly helpful if you've been finding yourself using anger as a mask for more vulnerable feelings that you're not ready or not willing to allow to come to the surface.

You can see how any one of these would be a

powerful angel to work with, and also how they can also be partnered and paired up to bring more depth to this work.

There are so many different ways you can work with your angels, but here are a few to get you started:

- Invite them into your meditation. When you sit down to meditate you can speak their name, or imagine their energy and invite it into your field. By meditating in their essence you will often feel more at peace, or receive the answers you need to the questions you haven't even yet asked.

- Pray to them. Whenever I pray to angels, I do so in trust. I ask in a way that is very declarative - I state what I'm seeking as though I'm assuming it's done and taken care of. (Because it is.) There is so much surrender in this process, that if you're even a little Type A may feel uncomfortable, but it's the language that has worked best with me as I work with them. You may ask something like "Thank you Archangel Haniel for helping me to understand the emotions I'm holding underneath this anger so that I may get to my heart's truth, and set myself free."

- Try automatic writing. This is a tool that a lot of Mediums use when communicating with the deceased, and I've found it very helpful in my practice when I'm accessing wisdom from other realms. I open up a notebook to a fresh page, ask the question I'm looking for answers to, and then set the intention that the question will be answered by the angel I know works with this area. Then comes trust... I loosely hold the pen in my dominant hand (other people will hold the pen in their non-dominant hand) and allow the words to pour out of me, onto the page. This isn't something that is only for Mediums, we all have intuitive gifts within us and so this is available to all. I also created a more visual doodle-y version of this process called art-o-matic writing. I've made the free guide downloadable in the sacred support bundle at sacredangerbook.com.

Crystals

Crystals and gemstones are minerals from the earth that contain different vibrational properties that are used in energetic healing and support. How they're made, what colour they are, and what elements they're composed of all have an impact on what kind of support they can bring to us as humans. When it comes to working with anger there are a few crystals I highly recommend:

Black Tourmaline – this is by far my favourite stone for transmuting any energy that we identify as heavy, so not only anger, but feelings like deep sadness, anxiety, frustration, and more.

Smoky Quartz – this stone is especially helpful when our anger is rooted in feelings of being unsafe, or unsupported. It's a very protective crystal that can help us to feel shielded as we work through our emotions.

Rose Quartz – whether you're needing to return to self, or tune into forgiveness, rose quartz is the stone holding a beautiful invitation to return to the heart. It's also the stone of self-love, so if you catch yourself being overly self-critical, and needing to return to love, this is the stone that will support you in getting there.

Carnelian - when you're doing the work of reclaiming your sense of self through therapy, anger management, and other reflective work to deal with unresolved emotions behind anger, carnelian is a beautiful support. It will help you cultivate a new trust in yourself to do things differently in the future.

Malachite is a powerful stone that brings everything to the surface.If you're having a hard time getting to what's underneath your anger, this is the stone that will help guide you. The only added warning I'll say though is that it has a tendency to amplify energy, so much like a detox, things may get worse before they get better because everything is now out in the open, ready to be dealt with.

Tiger's Eye - this stone brings objectivity and patience which are two of the biggest tools we can have when we're dealing with our anger, or the anger of others.

Alright, so now you have some ideas of what crystals to use, but you may be scratching your head about how to use them. While you can totally just hold them mindfully or sit with them in meditation, here are a few other ways to get started:

- Display them in your home or office. There are so many decorative pieces available now - raw or polished, shaped in spheres, eggs and wands, or in their more natural forms, that you can easily work them into your decor. Larger pieces can make beautiful book ends, sculptures, and paper weights.

- Wear them as jewelry. This is probably the most covert way to work with crystal energy. Having stones that are lovingly crafted in rings, necklaces, bracelets or Mala beads can be a wonderful way to bring the energy with you, and discreetly support yourself in even the most formal environments. I did make the distinction about crafted lovingly vs. Mass produced because I feel it's an important one to make. When something is crafted by hand by an artisan rather than mass produced in a factory with questionable standards and ethics, it can make such a difference in how the stone can support you. I've found many talented artists on Etsy who create beautiful and sometimes statement pieces, and I know they've been made with love, intention, and they understand the energy involved in their craft.

- Carry them in your pockets or your bra. I'd like to preface this with a warning to only do this with tumbled stones. (If you've ever held a piece of raw black tourmaline in your hand, you know what I'm talking about.) While the energy isn't drastically affected by a raw or tumbled stone, the physical sensations you'll experience will vary greatly. A tumbled stone feels smooth on the skin and won't destroy the fabric of your pockets. What's so lovely about this method of working with stones is that you can use smaller pieces, making it the least expensive and most discreet of all the methods.

- Use them in your sacred spaces. Whether it's an altar, or a crystal grid built with an intention, having them in the space that you use for meditation, reflection, and tapping into messages from your angels and guides have a beautiful way of bringing a new layer of energetic support.

No matter how you choose to work with your stones, you'll want to make sure you keep up their energetic maintenance. Clear the energy of your stones before you use them and after - especially if they've been helping you process something really big. You can do this by burning sage and running them through the smoke, putting them in the window (or outdoors) on the night of the full moon, or by burying them in the dirt or in a bowl of sea salt.

Essential Oils

Whether it's grounding your energy down, or returning to the heart, there's an essential oil for that. Here's the thing though, essential oils aren't for everyone. If you have a hard time with fragrances, even natural ones, or if you're in the early stages of pregnancy, or you're a child, essential oils should be avoided or used with extreme caution. Some oils can cause allergic reactions, and be toxic to pets, so you'll want to be careful.

All of this is to say - use high quality, therapeutic

grade oils from a trusted source, and find a certified aromatherapist to help you find the best ways to work with nature's medicine (and that's not your friend who has started selling essential oils from a multi level marketing company). And please, for the love of all things sparkly, don't eat your oils. <end rant>

Now that I've got that housekeeping out of the way, let's dive into the oils that can help you deal with your feels.

- **Need to get grounded?**
  Try a woody oil like sandalwood, rosewood, or cedar.
- **Need to get back to your heart?**
  Try oils like rose, jasmine, or geranium.
- **Need to relax and unwind?**
  Try soothing oils like lavender, chamomile, or frankincense.

You can use a diffuser or nebulizer to release the oils into a room (a nebulizer will keep the therapeutic properties most intact on a molecular level), you can have them in a room mist or a topical ointment, or you can dilute them in a good quality oil and apply them to your body - but don't apply them directly to your skin in an undiluted form. Essential oils are very potent plant medicine and often quite corrosive, so you can do a lot of damage if you don't dilute it first.

Make sure you're using an ethical supplier when you purchase your oils. Many crops have been over-harvested and there are now worldwide shortages happening around the world. If we're going to work with elements from nature, we need to do so with love and respect.

While different oils have been studied and noted for their emotional, psychological and physical properties, never underestimate your own experience. Smell is one of the biggest triggers of memory and emotion, so if you have a particular oil or oil combination that brings you back to a time where you felt really supported, it may not be the textbook recommendation, but still perfectly perfect for you.

Sacred Smoke

The burning of sacred smoke and passing it through your energy field or around a physical space that needs clearing has been an ancient tradition for Indigenous people around the world.

While it's become a common practice in Western society, it's important that we are respectful of where these traditions come from, mindful in how we use this work, and ethical in where we source our supplies as many are dwindling around the world.

Different cultures burn different items, symbolically, and for their cleansing properties. Sage seems to be the most commonly used plant for energy clearing in mainstream culture, making it the easiest to find in new age shops and even natural pharmacies. Other plants that are burned include sweet grass, tobacco, incense, resins and palo santo.

EFT (Emotional Freedom Technique)

EFT (also known as tapping) is an energetic system that works with the meridian system in the body, much in the same way as acupuncture and acupressure do. By tapping on these points, in a particular sequence, and speaking very personalized statements, you not only acknowledge what it is you're feeling, but also declaring self acceptance despite the occurrence of those feelings. As an example, you may say something like, "Even though I feel this anger coursing through my veins, I deeply and completely love and accept myself."

This technique has a beautiful way of getting us to speak up and honour our truth (no matter how ugly) so we can not only release it, but begin to create something new for ourselves. There are loads of guided tapping scripts and videos available online, but the more personalized you can make it (your feelings AND your words) the more effective it will be.

Mantras and Affirmations

Mantras and affirmations are statements that we can use to help bring about a particular feeling and outcome. On the surface they appear to be the same sort of thing – something you can say every day to tune in and call in. They can be used in meditation, as the thing you use to start and end your day with, or set on an alarm that you see at the same time every day. They can be sung, or chanted, or doodled. As with most things spiritual, the HOW is less important than the doing itself.

Though both are motivational, the main difference between mantras and affirmations is that mantras are devotional words (so you'll see these more in meditation, yoga, and even kirtan) and affirmations are inspirational words (so you'll see them more in manifestation work and as pep talks). You can see how both can support you when you're digging into emotional work.

Much like the language used in tapping with EFT, the more personal you can make it the more powerful it will be. The words need to feel like they are yours, and they should feel aligned to the outcome you're trying to create.

When using mantras and affirmations while working through anger you can decide to be grounded, open, or willing. Let your heart guide you.

When I've had a major outburst of anger and I'm sitting in the aftermath I'm often feeling very shaken up, and not fully in trust that it's over. It's all a bit raw and emotional and I feel completely depleted. I like to use this affirmation to help me return to centre and connect to my roots:

I am grounded.
I am supported.
I am rooted to the earth,
And protected by her love.

While I say it, I imagine myself as a tree that's recovering from a storm. The roots are holding me and grounding me to the earth, and even though I felt a bit blown by strong winds, at my core, I am supported and centred.

Speaking of grounding...

Grounding is a beautiful practice that gets us into our bodies and anchors our energy into the earth beneath us. Earthing, a grounding practice done by walking barefoot on the grass, has been studied by medical professionals and has been proven to reduce stress, pain, and inflammation in the body.

We've lost our connection to the earth, and grounding brings us back there. This connection is our natural state - it's the way things used to be and can be going forward.

Everyone has a favourite way to ground their energy. Earthing is a practice adored by many, but even just being in nature, slowing the breath, hugging a tree, and meditating can help us to center our energy, and send it to the earth. Root vegetables, dark chocolate, base chakra meditations, and dark crystals like black tourmaline, hematite, and red jasper can all help us ground our energy as well.

Grounding isn't just a mindful practice to bring us back to ourselves, it's the way home when we've been in a state of chaos (our own, or others). It's how we can return to the heart when things have been overwrought or out of control. It's the journey home to the sacred self.

Hand it over to a higher power

I wanted to call this section 'surrender', but if you're anything like me, that word creates a TON of resistance within you. I want to feel in charge of my own destiny, like a powerful creator of my existence, so the idea of just letting go to let God do their thing kind of stressed me out a little if I'm honest.

That's because I wasn't in a space of trust.

When we try to do everything on our own, including navigating through our emotions, we are limited. Sometimes being strong, capable and independent is actually a disservice. When we've done all that we can do, and then we hand over the rest to a higher power there is such liberation in this act. It moves us beyond what we can create on our own (which, because we're limited human beings, can only be so much) into a state of possibility and openness. We aren't limited by our own perception, or the lens we view the world in – EVERYTHING is possible. Our scope and perspective is widened and we can receive so much more than we could've created on our own.

I know a lot of people have been hurt by organized religion, and this can create a crisis of faith, or turn people into non-believers. If the word God doesn't work for you, but you find the angels, guides, Universe, Source, etc to be more supportive, then use that word instead. If you don't believe at all, but you can lean into the knowingness that you've done the best you could and that has to be enough, then that's where this can take you.

SACRED SOUL SEARCHING

Here are the reflection questions to take to your journal:

What are the ways I can support my body when I'm feeling angry?

What are the ways I can support my emotional and energetic states when I'm feeling angry?

What new strategies am I feeling called to explore, and why?

CHAPTER 10
Reclaiming your power

When we examine anger, we're often looking for strategies to defeat it. Courtrooms will dispense orders for anger management classes, spiritual teachers will focus on the abolition of the ego so that it's no longer navigating life for you, and marketers will have you believe that if you buy another retreat, another course, another certification, you'll have it all figured out.

And then there's this book telling you how to learn from it as a sacred teacher and tool.

The common thread that strings these all together is that we want to learn new ways to reclaim our power - because whatever is causing the anger, or whatever is happening underneath it, has left us feeling like we didn't have a say in how it all unfolds.

In this chapter we're going to look at some ways you can begin the process of reclaiming your power so that you can reap the benefits of working with your anger, and start to recover from it more quickly.

Peace begins with boundaries.

One of the biggest things that pisses women off is when they feel tread on, taken for granted, and taken advantage of. A huge part of this comes from our conditioning to be nice and to people please, which leaves our own priorities and needs pushed to the back of the queue, which means we get resentful of tending to everyone else's happiness first. I don't say this to victim blame here, there are also legitimate cases where people are assholes who tread upon whatever boundaries are set, but in general, the reason people don't honour our boundaries is because we're taught not to set them in the first place.

I'm the first to admit that I've compromised myself more often than is comfortable to see. In friendships, partnerships, with family, with lovers, with work... there's been an imbalance in the energies invested and a lot of it came from not just unspoken desires to be seen/heard/accepted/desired, but also the unspoken expectation that they'd just figure it out and do things differently, even though it had always been that way.

Boundaries are fierce declarations of self love.

They declare you are worthy and deserving of your heart's desire. (Hint: YOU ARE.) They're also challenging to the parts of you that believe otherwise, and these parts will push back whenever you take a stand for yourself. Because it's a lot easier to be angry at someone on the outside than to address the internal tug of war that says "I deserve this. No I don't."

Boundaries aren't about keeping people out. They're about creating space so you have more to give.

When we start to take care of ourselves, we are happier, healthier, and have more energy to support the people and causes we care about. We can't do any of that well (without burning out) if we don't make time and devote some energy and space to our own work. This isn't about taking a weekly bubble bath and calling it self care. I mean doing work like examining your anger, moving your body, creating mindfulness practices, drinking water and getting enough sleep. This isn't self love propaganda funded by the bubble bath brigade... it's the fundamentals required to show up for the people we love (including ourselves.) It all begins with you.

Here's the tricky thing about boundaries... we often don't know what they are until we've crossed them. Because we aren't taught to look at our priorities, or uphold boundaries, or put our needs first, it can be so easy to push through something and regret it later. (Think of the late nights at the office that meant missing your child's Christmas concert. Or roleplaying a fantasy with a lover that you didn't feel much about at the start, but felt icky at the end.)

It's impossible to expect perfection from ourselves.

Sometimes we will get it wrong. And when we do, it may feel awful - not just angry, but also shameful, disappointed, sad, a million other unpleasant things. The feelings are entirely valid - don't deny them. Just make sure to pick yourself back up and move forward after.

All you can do, at any given time, is your best. And what constitutes your 'best' will vary from one moment to the next.

Breathe that in for a second. Doesn't it take some of the pressure off?

If I'm doing my best at any given time, and I allow my boundaries to be walked on, it's the best that was possible for me to do in that moment. I can learn from that, grow from that so I do things differently next time, and I can forgive myself for not being able to honour me differently in that moment. And that's where it can end. It doesn't have to be bigger, or more dramatic. It's the start of a new chapter of honouring myself in new and better ways that are evolving as I do. Boundary work isn't something you 'set and forget'. It's a garden you tend to that grows as you give it time, attention, and love.

NO is a sacred word

As a recovering people pleaser, I found it hard to use 'no' as a standalone statement, without the need to explain or justify it. But honouring the word "no" is a natural extension from the boundary conversation.

"No." is a complete sentence, if you choose to use it that way.

If you're like me, and find yourself a bit queasy about saying no a whole lot more than you do now, allow me to offer you this reframing: saying no to this allows you to say yes to something else. (Even if that something else is a cup of tea and your favourite show on Netflix.)

When we say "yes" to stuff that doesn't light us up we start to build up resentment, we start to get tired, we get irritable and we get angry. Overscheduling your life (to please others, to distract from feelings you want to avoid, to create the illusion of a life you're not actually living) is not the key to happiness - doing more of what you love is. Every undeserving "yes" comes at a price to our time, attention, and energy... we just often can't see it until the bill comes due. Suddenly all of those undeserving yeses stop feeling like easy things you could do to make somebody happy, and you can feel the burden they create within you.

This is particularly hard when we start to define our worth based on our achievements (whether it's a big salary, a big house, a spouse, children, whatever). We trick ourselves into believing that the million little yeses we've said are temporary sacrifices to get what we want in life, so they seem worth it at the time. This is probably the biggest lie we tell ourselves, for a couple of reasons.

Firstly: the life you actually want is not built on the stuff you surround yourself with, or any other superficial change. That's momentary joy from instant gratification - not a fulfilling and happy life. If your stuff truly brings joy, it's likely fulfilling something underneath.

Secondly: when we're basing our worth on something outside of ourselves, there is no such thing as temporary sacrifice. Our shadow self will just keep moving the happiness target to "just one more thing" until we've completely lost ourselves in the quest for more.

When I worked in corporate, I was initially hired at a higher rate as a consultant. When I was brought on as an employee my salary was reduced but came with vacation and benefits. However when I had my first salary review, the proposed salary was still lower than my original rate, despite having done the job with great success for over a year and a half. My personal circumstances had changed - I was raising my younger sister and, frankly, I needed the money to be able to rent a bigger apartment for the two of us. When I made the case for the higher salary (a difference of $3K a year) I was told that if I wanted more, I'd need to make it up in commission. The thing is, I wasn't asking for the additional money (and offered to forego commission) because I was striving for more, but because I'd tied up my own worth in being able to provide for my sister, and in being valued by my employer. (I was constantly hungry for an atta girl from the owners of the company.) Additionally, I was asked to look at the strategic value I brought to the company. The owner said "By that I mean, if you were hit by a bus tomorrow, how hard would it be for us to replace you?"

It's been 14 years and those words still sting.

Not only was my performance not enough to help me provide for my family, there was no pat on the back for the work I was doing well, and suddenly the responsibilities I had kept me from walking out of that meeting (and that job). I felt powerless on top of it all and spent the rest of the review angrily crying in front of my superiors, defeated. (Although I did get great satisfaction when they paid me over $10k in additional commission that year.)

There will be times when you can't honour your

"no", it would be naive and hypocritical of me to tell you to just walk out of that meeting and burn your career to the ground if they don't appreciate you, because I didn't, and I didn't feel I could. So in those times where outside circumstances are forcing a "yes" (not where you've talked yourself into one - think losing your job vs volunteering for the PTA), recognize the choice. Feel whatever comes up because your hand was forced, and start making a plan so that you can prevent this from becoming your new normal. You may not be able to honour your no in that moment, but you can make future decisions that will keep you from having to compromise it time and time again.

Your pain as a catalyst for change

There is a lot of pressure from our societal conditioning to make things seem really good all the time - which means we diminish anything that feels less than good, often pretending it's not happening at all. When you run into someone on the street, how often have you honestly answered "How's it going?" when you weren't having a great day? 'Fine' becomes a social handshake, rather than an accurate expression of how we're feeling at the time.

Same goes for the photos and stories we share on social media. I understand that there's a time and a place to have these conversations, and everyone has different comfort levels with sharing vulnerably. I'm not saying you should pour your heart out to strangers on the street, but I am inviting you to consider how truthfully you show up in the world, and look at where you can bring more heart and more honesty to your sharing.

I can't tell you how often I've received messages from people on Facebook who I'm connected to but haven't actually spoken to in 20+ years who will ask me about my struggles with anxiety and body positivity. Because while they may not have been engaging with me, they were watching. And because I shared openly and honestly, I created a safe space for them to talk about everything they were experiencing. In some cases, I was literally the only person they knew they could reach out to because no one else was having those conversations. You don't have to end up on Oprah's book club for your story to be helpful. Showing up authentically has an impact on the people closest to you, and it has a ripple effect that reaches farther than you can likely imagine.

Sacred Activism

Much like the people mentioned in Chapter 2, there are ways to put our pain and our anger to work for us. Whether it's making a movement like Greta Thunberg, the teenager environmental activist from Sweden, or writing a memoir like Elizabeth Gilbert's "Eat, Pray, Love", or even just sharing honestly and openly on social media or at family gatherings. When you share your journey, you help other people who are going through the same thing feel less alone, less weird, and less cast out.

We don't want pain to be the only thing that unites us. But if it can be the thing that initially brings us together, starts the conversations happening, and leads to eventual change, then it wasn't in vain.

How can you put your anger to work for you? Are there causes you can volunteer for? Petitions you can sign? Charities you can donate to? Look for different ways to show up for the things that make you feel the fire in your belly - and if you can't find them, start them. This is how you transform those feelings of powerlessness into knowing you can conquer just about anything, especially when you're surrounded by people who share the same cause.

Get real about what you feel

If there is one thing that happens with literally every single one of my coaching clients, it's learning to examine what's behind our behaviour. Because it's not just anger that we avoid dealing with or mislabeling, it's pretty much anything that's uncomfortable - even when it's supporting our growth. This was the inspiration behind my podcast, The Lightwalker's Path. I was witnessing a lot of "airy fairy" conversations about what it meant to live and build a spiritual life, and not a lot of the actual work that took place.

This "love and light" approach is a type of spiritual bypassing - it's sidestepping the actual work that needs to be done, but doing so with spiritual language, so you sound like you're doing the work when really, you're just talking about it. One of the people I interviewed is my friend George Lizos, and he said "It's not lightwork, it's light chilling." and he's absolutely right. Worse than the mislabeling though, for the people who were actually doing the work who were looking up to these "light chillers", is that they felt they were doing things wrong, or that they were to blame for their struggles, because no one was being honest about the journey.

Here's the truth: it doesn't matter who you are, what mantras you say, how much yoga you do or how cleanly you eat.... There will be bad days, they will happen, they will challenge you. But, when you do this work, how you manage those bad days, and how you recover from them will change drastically.

And it all begins with being honest about what you're actually feeling.

We have so much judgment about our feelings, especially those of us who've been on a spiritual path for awhile. We label them as good/bad, high/low vibe, light/dark, and it's all just bullshit. They're just feelings, just energy, and sticking them into a box doesn't make them easier to cope with - it just creates more of a story, and more drama for us to glom onto instead of actually experiencing them and all they're trying to teach us.

The stories and the drama are wonderful distractions from actually doing the work. It's one of the most genius shadow tactics we'll experience. So long as we are prisoners to our emotions, or we treat them as puzzles that need to be figured out, we aren't actually learning and moving forward. We've once again handed over our power, and now something else is in the driver's seat of our lives – whether it's the emotion itself, or the distraction (or the whispering shadow self who is puppeteering all of this).

Choosing to sit with an emotion, instead of treating it as something that needs to be understood, sounds like a passive task, but it's actually very deliberate, and a very conscious choice. It's not easy stuff, even when the emotion is joyful. It requires a keen eye, an open heart, and a willingness to witness without trying to analyze, fix, or change anything. And that's powerful AF. You will learn so much more, and grow so much more through this detached witnessing of your emotions than you will by calling the CSI squad with their ultraviolet lights to do a forensic investigation of your feelings.

Honestly gauging where you're at and what you feel is the best way to deepen your connection to yourself, your soul, and your purpose. It becomes easier to honour your inner voice and knowing because you can hear it with so much more clarity, and you can trust it to lead the way.

We're nearing the end of our time together here, so I'd like to leave you with this final thought: none of the work that's been described in this book – the reflection, the inner exploration, the honest talks... none of it can help you get to your heart's truth if you aren't willing to stick with it. I say this with zero judgment, because we're all on different journeys. Sometimes the time isn't right, you're too worried about the consequences, or you're feeling fearful of what's next. Where you're at is exactly right.

Here's the thing, Lovely: you are the ultimate decider of all the things in your life. It's your very own Choose Your Own Adventure novel, and you get to pick how you want this to feel.

The beauty about learning things is that once we know them we can't "unknow" them. So even if the timing isn't right, the seeds have been planted and they'll be ready when you are.

This is your invitation, my sweet... to choose... to commit... It doesn't have to be to this particular work, but it does need to be something. And when you do, show up for it, even if it's for just 5 minutes a day, regularly. What you do doesn't matter as much as how you do it. Be conscious with it, be intentional, and allow it to nourish you so much that it becomes a non-negotiable part of your routine.

This way of intentionally living brings more connection, more depth, more heart to every word, thought and action. It starts to create a new reality for you - one where you are firmly planted in the driver's seat, being guided by a GPS you can trust, where you have total control over the vehicle. You're driving it, it's not driving you. You're aware of your surroundings, you can see alternate routes to consider, and you are living with more power and purpose than ever before.

The journey is waiting for you... I can't wait to see where you'll go!

SACRED SOUL SEARCHING

Here are the reflection questions to take
to your journal:

*What actions can you take to put your
anger to work for you?*

*Now that we know anger is an indicator
of what you value, and what's most
important to you, what is YOUR anger
trying to teach you?*

EPILOGUE

I did it. I wrote the book about anger that I told everyone I was working on. And for the most part I feel like I've won a round with the shadow self, but then I'm immediately humbled by my human side that still has the occasional dance with anger.

Which takes us to now...

Halloween 2020. I'm in the home stretch of writing this book and have spent the last 2.5 years immersed in the exploration of anger. It's already been a dumpster fire of a year and I've noticed my patience is thinner than it used to be. (Maybe because I turned 40 this year? #theories #oldladythoughts.)

It's 1am and someone in my neighbourhood is STILL shooting off fireworks. They've woken me several times. My nervous system is processing them as gunshots. I am not the happiest camper.

Mentally I start drafting a Facebook post that I'm too tired to actually write:

How to deal with the assholes who are still shooting off fireworks at 1am:

Step 1: build a time machine. Go back to a time pre-pandemic and invest in a pellet gun and some lessons in marksmanship. Invest the time to get really good. Maybe also some laser eye surgery so you can see better at night.

Step 2: fly back to present day. Before going to bed, remove your bedroom window screen. Wait.

Step 3: when the sounds get louder and closer, grab your pellet gun, lean out your window, and shoot those little fuckers in the ass. Do it as many times as necessary for them to get the idea to move along.

Step 4: if step 3 takes too long, repeat step 1 but bring some neighbours with you so you can do it together.

Friend, this is after nearly 15 years of really deep inner work and a lifetime of learning to work with my anger.

I'm not asking you to become some kind of zen master who doesn't have angry thoughts. To this day, whenever I feel threatened or someone I love has been hurt, my inner Ruth Langmore hops into the driver's seat for a joyride. But she's mostly talk, she helps me blow off some steam so I don't implode. When it's not her, sometimes it's ridiculous time travel fantasies to escape from a situation momentarily.

The goal is not to stop feeling angry.

To do this would deny you some ultra rich life lessons and probably make you pretty miserable. Instead, I want you to experience the depth of life's lessons, including uncomfortable emotions like anger, so you can learn and grow and support your soul's expansion.

We need your light in this world.

Let's not dim it by allowing anger to consume you when you could burn so much brighter by treating it as a sacred teacher and learning all she has to offer you.

CONTINUE YOUR JOURNEY

When I first started on my spiritual path in 2008, no one told me that I was beginning a lifelong journey. Inner work is a lot like toothpaste – once it's out, it's really hard to put back in. But here's the thing: you're not alone. So many people are like you, beginning their journey with anger, mindfulness, or even asking questions about what it all means.

If you're at this point and wondering what to do next, here's the best place to start:

Sacred supports

If you haven't already, make sure you download all of the resources I've put together to help you deepen the work outlined in this book. You can find them all at sacredangerbook.com.

Stay connected

I send a weekly email to my community with little nuggets I'm learning on my spiritual path, and with early access to the events and offers I release. Bonus: you'll get to download my free PDF, The Lightwalker's Path to Energy Management which will give you some of my favourite tools to move and transmute energy (including anger). Sign up at seryna.ca/energy-management.

Dig deeper

This book is a pretty clear indicator of my approach to coaching. (Direct, no nonsense, but also deeply intuitive and filled with love.) In my practice, I guide helpers, healers and high achievers get real about their heart's desire, so they can live with more power and more purpose. I have 1:1 packages and group programs for those that prefer social learning. You can learn about my latest offerings at www.seryna.ca.

Find your peeps

I host a sweet community of people on Facebook who are digging into their inner work (anger and so much more!) and looking for somewhere safe to share about their process. If you're looking for your peeps, I'd love to introduce you to mine. You can find them in Facebook Groups under The Lightwalker's Path.

Stay inspired

Speaking of The Lightwalker's Path, it's also the name of my podcast. In it, we have raw, real and honest conversations about what it actually means to live a spiritual life. Episodes tend to be under a half hour, so they're easy to squeeze into any day. You can listen and subscribe on all major platforms, including Apple Podcasts and Spotify.

Keep in touch

On social media, you'll find me as @serynamyers on Facebook and Instagram. I'd love to cheer you on from afar, so tag me in your posts about your work with anger so I can pull out my pom poms to celebrate you.

ACKNOWLEDGEMENTS

This book has been a labour of love, but also at times a lot of work. I'm so grateful to everyone and everything (including my therapist and my anti-depressants) who kept me afloat through this process:

To my beloved, I know anger isn't your favourite topic and still, you held space and supported me through all of this - including the anger that came up within me. Thank you for making me a mom, and for all the lessons that brought - even the hard ones. Words can't express how much you mean to me, and how grateful I am to you for all that you are, and all that you do. (Even the stuff you think I don't notice... because I do.)

To my writing mentors, George and Tesa, thank you for helping me get all of this stuff in my head that built up from a lifetime of experience with anger, and turn it into a cohesive vision that will go on to support people long after I'm gone. I couldn't have done it without your wisdom, your know-how, and your cheerleading.

To my publisher, That Guy's House, thank you for giving me a platform to share what I've learned, and especially to Leah for making this book so damn beautiful.

To my editor Rhea, who I trust with these words, and so much more. Thank you for helping me find the best ways to articulate these lessons, and for catching any typos that come from typing over 100wpm. Your eagle eye is only one of the many things I adore about you.

To the friends and family whose stories I've shared, but especially my dad and my brother Chad... I can't imagine it was easy for you to let me talk about these painful times, and still, you gave me your blessing so our past pain could help heal the collective anger wound. I am awestruck at your generosity and so so SO grateful for the courage it took for you to say yes.

To the women in my life who've been there through some of my angriest times: Zoë, Richelle, Juliana, Kari, Keyla, Tanya, Lauren, Michelle S., Michelle B., Nicole S. and Nicole D... And Shawn (who gets an honourable mention despite being a dude): you have created space throughout some of the most challenging parts of my journey for me to reflect, to vent and to gain perspective. I've always felt held and loved, and never felt judged. Your friendship has been a balm for my soul.

And lastly, to Dr. Brené Brown, who doesn't know me, but who has inspired so much of my personal and professional work. My journey with anger began as a purely spiritual one, but your teachings have helped me anchor it here on Earth. Thank you for your courage and vulnerability – I am forever changed because of your work.

ABOUT THE AUTHOR

Seryna Myers is a spiritual teacher, author and transformational speaker. She is the voice behind The Lightwalker's Path podcast and online community, and host of intimate spiritual retreats.

She creates safe and sacred spaces to have honest conversations with yourself about who you are and how you really feel. Her coaching guides the helpers, healers and high achievers of the world tap into their divine gifts and share them through their lives and leadership.

Seryna makes her home on the west coast of Canada with her beautiful husband and their cats.